Marcus Fayette Cummings

Architecture

Designs for street fronts, suburban houses, and cottages. including details, for both

exterior and interior, of the above classes of buildings

Marcus Fayette Cummings

Architecture
Designs for street fronts, suburban houses, and cottages. including details, for both exterior and interior, of the above classes of buildings

ISBN/EAN: 9783337149444

Printed in Europe, USA, Canada, Australia, Japan

Cover: Foto ©Thomas Meinert / pixelio.de

More available books at **www.hansebooks.com**

ARCHITECTURE.

DESIGNS

FOR

STREET FRONTS, SUBURBAN HOUSES,

AND

COTTAGES,

INCLUDING DETAILS, FOR BOTH EXTERIOR AND INTERIOR, OF THE ABOVE CLASSES OF
BUILDINGS. ALSO, A GREAT VARIETY OF DETAILS NOT INCLUDED IN
THE DESIGNS, ILLUSTRATED BY ELEVATIONS.

AND CONTAINING IN ALL OVER 1,000 DESIGNS AND ILLUSTRATIONS.

EDITED BY

CUMMINGS & MILLER,

AUTHORS OF "MODERN AMERICAN ARCHITECTURE."

SIXTH THOUSAND.

A. J. BICKNELL & CO., ARCHITECTURAL BOOK PUBLISHERS,
TROY, N. Y., AND SPRINGFIELD, ILLS.
1868.

Lithographed and Printed by

JULIUS BIEN,

New York.

INTRODUCTION.

MANY architectural works have been published in our country, which treat more or less of street architecture, country houses, villas, and domestic architecture generally, in which are given plans, elevations, and perspective views of buildings of all kinds. Many of these works are highly meritorious, and it would be well for the taste of the people, if they were more generally circulated and studied.

The illustrations in the works referred to, though they portray many beautiful buildings and well arranged plans, are almost invariably drawn to so small a scale as to render comprehending their details, impossible to any one except experienced architects.

To arrange the rooms and appurtenances of a building in accordance with a given diagram is not a difficult task, even though the scale of the diagram be very small; but to erect a building, and to make all the details of its exterior and interior finish beautiful, and to have each detail such that it will aid in forming a harmonious whole, requires for a guide something more elaborated than an illustration in perspective, such as can be found in nearly all of the architectural works published in this country.

This work differs in its design from any, heretofore issued; it contains designs for all the various features which enter into the composition of buildings, both for the city and for the country, and these features are again given in detail, and drawn to so large a scale that any one familiar with the construction of work cannot fail to comprehend their forms and their construction. In addition to these, there are given a variety of elevations of fronts of buildings in which the details are incorporated, thereby showing their effect when combined, forming a whole.

This work treats of none of the orders or styles of architecture; information in regard to them can be derived from other sources: from standard works and from architects whose reputation is a sufficient guarantee of their competency, and any one who desires to incorporate the features of any particular style in a building they propose to erect, should procure complete designs and drawings from an architect of known ability.

No plans of houses are given in this work, for the reason, that the wants of persons in regard to the arrangements of their buildings are as different as are their characters; and to present plans within the small compass of a book that would suit even a respectable minority of those who build every year would be an impossibility.

The elevations given are such as may be applied to the ordinary outlines of buildings, such as are frequently adopted in this country. The designs and details of the various features given are so extensive and so varied in their character, that they can be applied with success to any structures except public buildings. Judgment must be used in the selection, and to guide that, it will be proper to study well the elevations given, in which the effect of the details can be seen and appreciated.

This work will be found particularly valuable in situations where it is not convenient to secure the services of an architect; in such localities owners and their builders are usually thrown upon their own resources of knowledge, as to what is good and in proper taste to introduce into the design of the building they propose to erect: and if they possess a work in which every needed architectural feature, both those of utility and those of ornament, is given, necessary to the complete construction of the building, it will not be a difficult task to make the structure a good-proportioned and inviting one.

Without such a work, the only alternative is either to engage an architect or to follow in the footsteps of some predecessor, copy his building as far as is practicable, and so add one more to the many generations of nondescripts and "scenery disturbers," which mar our beautiful country everywhere, in localities distant from our chief cities. That the work will be deemed valuable, when examined, and found of great service, when used, is the belief of the authors: and that it may do much to correct evils at present existing in building operations, and elevate and aid the taste of those who build, is their earnest wish.

M. F. CUMMINGS, } AUTHORS.
C. C. MILLER,

Plate 1

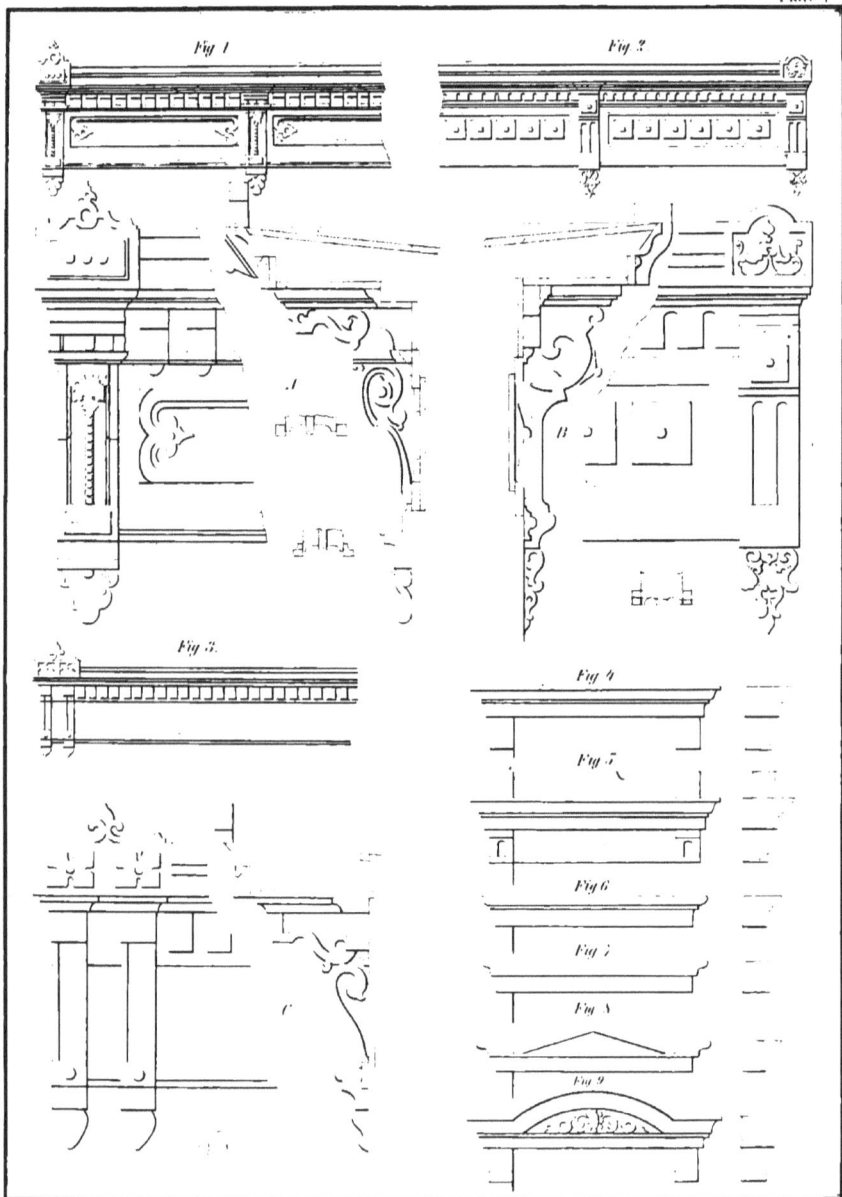

Fig 1

Fig 2

Fig 3

Fig 4

Fig 5

Fig 6

Fig 7

Fig 8

Fig 9

· P L A T E 1.

Fig. 1. Shows a cornice having trusses, which are moulded on the face and enriched with carved leaves and beads. Over the trusses are moulded modillions, and over the end trusses and modillions are end-blocks, having raised panels and surmounted by scrolls 4 inches thick. Between the trusses are panels, having mouldings at the top and bottom and sawed scrolls at the ends. Over the panels are dentils, sawed to a mould on the face. At A are the details of the cornice, comprising an elevation and section, and sections of the face of the trusses and modillions.

Fig. 2. Shows a cornice having trusses, fluted on the face, enriched at the foot and panelled at the top. Between the trusses are sunk panels in the frieze, and in these are raised blocks with balls in the centre. The end-blocks are panelled and enriched. Over the frieze panels are sawed dentils, 3 inches thick. At B are the details, comprising an elevation and section of the cornice, and a section of the trusses.

Fig. 3. Shows a cornice having sawed trusses with modillions placed over them. The end-block has sawed rosettes and top scrolls. The frieze is plain, and over it are plain dentils. At C is a section and elevation of the cornice and a section of the trusses.

Figs. 4, 5, 6, 7, 8, and 9. Show elevations and sections of window caps.

The cornices shown at Figs. 1 and 2 are designed for buildings three stories in height, and the cornice shown at Fig. 3 is designed for a building two stories high. The end-blocks should be used where the cornice cannot extend around the building. The window-caps may be executed in stone, cast-iron, or wood; if of wood, they should be covered with tin on the top.

All details on this plate are drawn to a scale of ¾ of an inch to the foot; the designs are drawn to a scale of ¼ inch to the foot.

PLATE 2.

Fig. 1. Shows a cornice having enriched and moulded trusses, having moulded caps. The end-blocks are panelled and enriched, and have top scrolls. Between the trusses are moulded frieze panels, and over them are sawed modillions. At A is an elevation and section of cornice, side of modillions and section of trusses.

Fig. 2. Shows a cornice having trusses made of five thicknesses of plank. The foot leaves are sawed and have raised balls. The trusses have moulded caps and are enriched with carved rosettes. The end-blocks are fluted and have top scrolls. The frieze is panelled with raised mouldings, and over the panels are sawed dentils 3 inches thick. At B is an elevation and section of the cornice and a section of the trusses.

Fig. 3. Shows a cornice having modillions, and a sawed ornament in the frieze. At C are the details.

Fig. 4. Shows a cornice having sawed brackets, 6 inches thick, placed in pairs. At D are the details.

Fig. 5. Shows a cornice having brackets 6 inches thick, having turned drops, and raised panels. The frieze is panelled, and over it are plain dentils.

The cornices shown at Figs. 1 and 2 are designed for buildings three stories in height; those shown at Figs, 3, 4, and 5, for buildings two stories in height.

All designs in this plate are drawn to a scale of ¼ inch to the foot; the details are ¾ of an inch to the foot.

Plate 2

Fig. 1

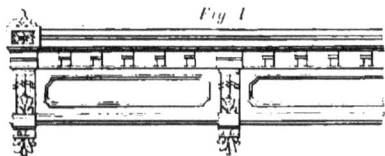

Fig. 2

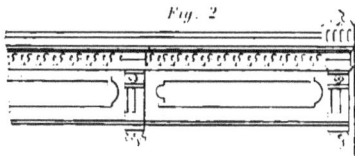

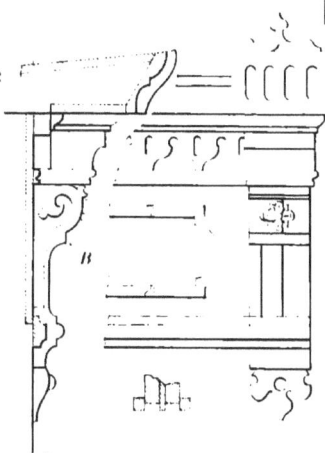

Fig. 3

Fig. 4

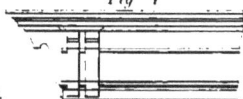

Fig. 5

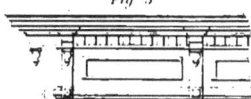

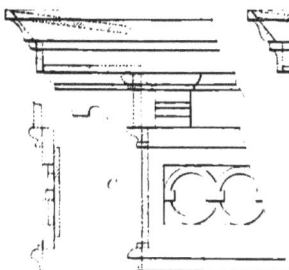

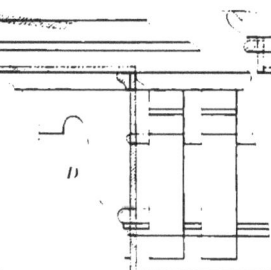

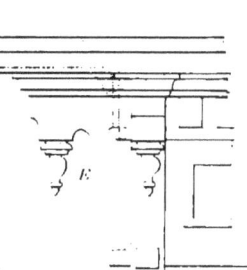

.

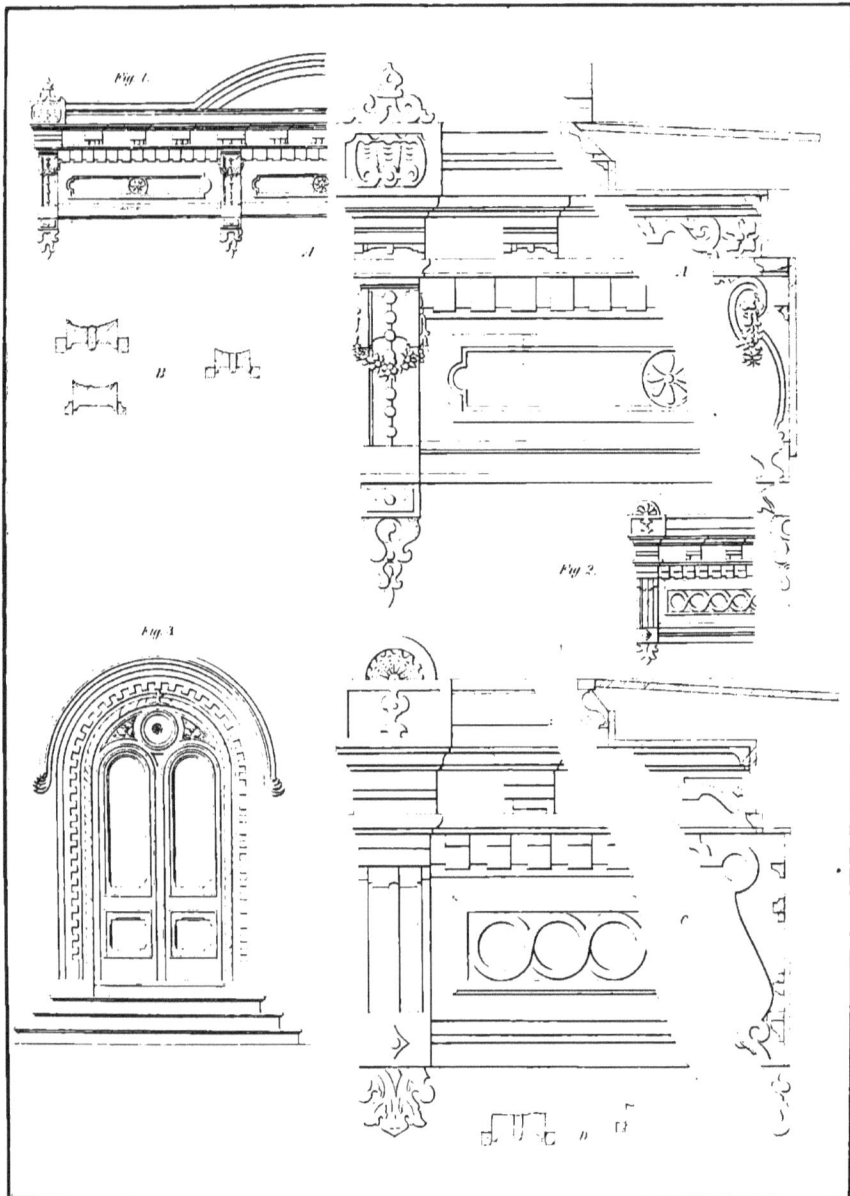

Plate 3

Fig. 1.

Fig. 2.

B

A

Fig. 3

B

PLATE 3.

Fig. 1. Shows a cornice having carved and moulded trusses elaborately enriched. The end-blocks are carved and have top scrolls. Over the trusses are moulded modillions, and like modillions are placed over the frieze. The frieze is panelled and moulded, and rosettes are placed in the centre of the panels. Over the panels are dentils, and the cornice is formed into a pediment in the centre. At A is a section and elevation of the cornice, and at B are shown sections of the face of the trusses and modillions.

Fig. 2. Shows a cornice having moulded and enriched trusses, with caps. The end-blocks are panelled and enriched. The frieze is panelled, and in the panels are sawed chain ornaments. Over the panels are dentils and sawed modillions. At C is shown an elevation and section of the cornice, and at D sections of the trusses and modillions.

The cornices on this plate should be used in buildings which are four or more stories in height.

The cornices shown in Plates 1, 2, and 3, are designed for buildings having fronts of from 20 feet to 30 feet wide; those having the bold trusses should have one truss to each pier; those that are shown at Figs. 4 and 5, on Plate 2, should have the brackets placed from 3 feet to 5 feet apart. The pediment shown in Fig. 1. Plate 3, may be introduced with good effect in any of the designs of cornices shown.

Fig. 3, on Plate 3, shows a design for a doorway, having brick joints, moulded stone hood, and carved wood frame. This doorway would make an appropriate entrance for a chapel or church of moderate expense.

The details of the cornices on this plate are drawn to a scale of $\frac{3}{4}$ of an inch to the foot, and the doorway to a scale of $\frac{1}{4}$ inch to the foot. The designs of the cornices are also drawn $\frac{1}{4}$ inch to the foot.

PLATE 4.

On this plate are shown four designs of cornices to be constructed of plain or common brick. The upper moulded members of the cornices and balustrades should be of cut stone or of wood; if of wood, they should be tinned on the top.

Fig. 1. Shows an elevation and section of a cornice having brackets 8 inches thick, and between them are sunk panels. The balustrade is 8 inches thick, with openings made through it. At the corners of the building should be plain pilasters.

Fig. 2. Shows a cornice having corbel arches at the bottom, projecting 4 inches from the wall. The frieze has arched recesses 8 inches deep. The balustrade is pierced with square panels.

Fig. 3. Shows a cornice having blocks 8 inches on the face, and projecting as shown on the section. At the corners of the building are placed pilasters, cut into blocks by receiving every sixth course of brick. The balustrade is pierced with openings, with piers between them.

Fig. 4. Shows a cornice having a frieze formed of intersecting arches, terminating on corbels; under the arches are panels and above them are corbelled projections. The balustrade is plain. The cornices shown on this plate are drawn to a scale of ¼ inch to a foot.

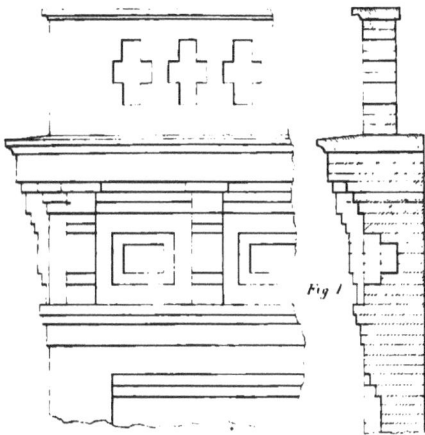

Fig 1

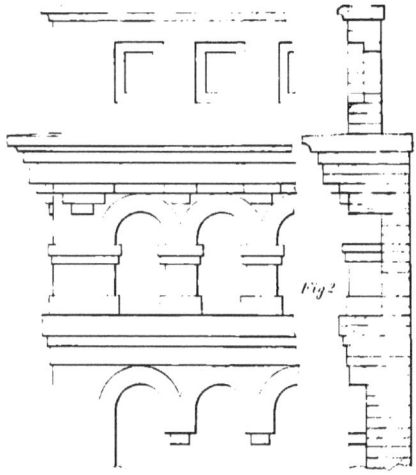

Fig 2

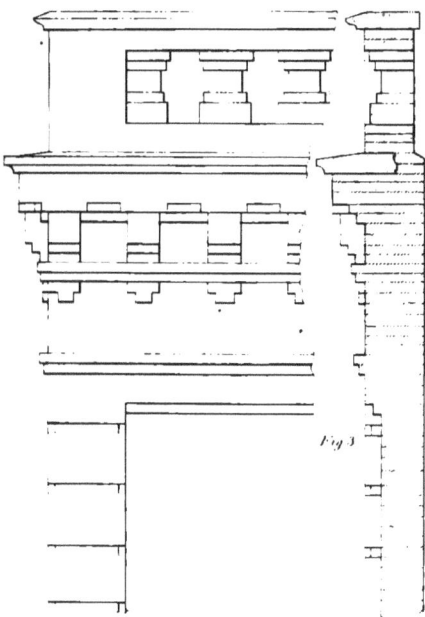

Fig 3

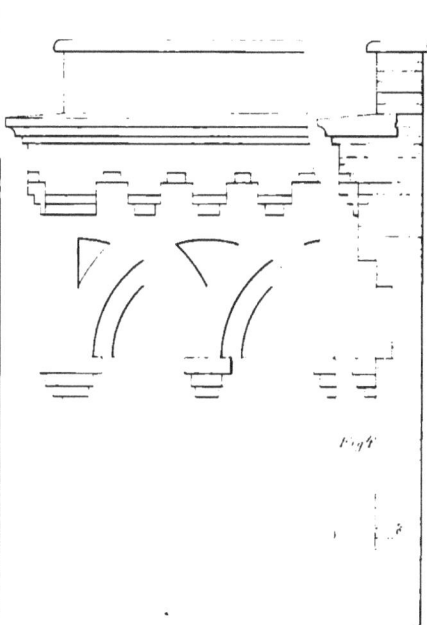

Fig 4

Plate 5.

Fig. 1.

Fig. 2.

A

B

C

D

E

F

G

H

PLATE 5.

Fig. 1. Has posts and lintels of wood or iron, chamfered at the corners, and the posts have vases and caps; those at the ends are also fluted in the centre. Brackets with panelled end-blocks are placed over the end-posts, and have top scrolls. The sills of the windows are moulded, and under them, and in the doors, are raised, chamfered and moulded panels. The details at A, show an elevation and section of the cornice, cap of centre-posts and section of sills and panels under the windows.

Fig. 2. Has panelled and enriched columns of cast-iron. The cornice and lintels may be of wood or iron. The cornice has enriched trusses over the end columns, and between them are modillions. The end-blocks are panelled and enriched. The door and window frames are arched and secured to the iron columns. The windows have moulded sills and panels under them. The details show sections and elevations of the cornice, columns, window-sills, and panels,—capital and enrichments of columns, and a side view of the modillions. This front should be used in a building possessing a good architectural character, and are of medium cost. Fig. 1, shows a front for a building of moderate expense.

The details on this plate are drawn to a scale of ¼ of an inch to the foot.

PLATE 6.

Fig. 1. Shows a front having the end piers of stone cut into rustic blocks. The columns should be of cast-iron, and the lintels and cornice of cut stone. Over the end piers are trusses and panelled end-blocks. The frames or posts of the doors are placed back of the columns and piers. The top of the openings are arched, and the spandrels are enriched with carved work; also the panels in the doors. At A are shown the columns and piers in elevation, and at C a plan of the same.

Fig. 2. Shows a front which should be constructed of stone. The columns have moulded vases and caps; the frieze is arched, and over the openings are hood mouldings. The cornice is moulded and has end-blocks. The frames of the doors are attached to the stone piers. At D are sections of the piers and doors, and at B, elevations of the piers.

The details on this plate are drawn to a scale of ¾ of an inch to a foot

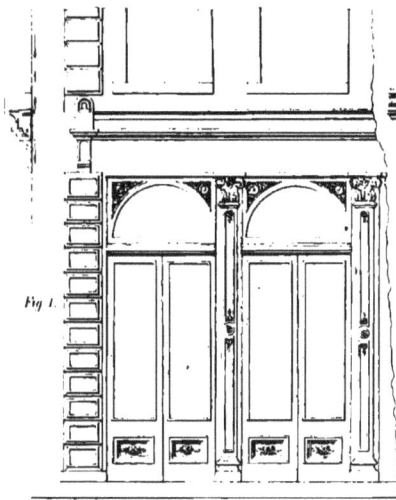

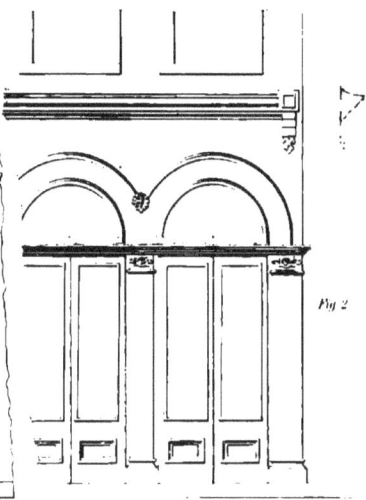

Fig 1.

Fig 2.

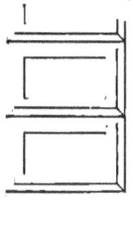

A

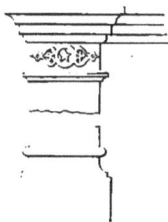

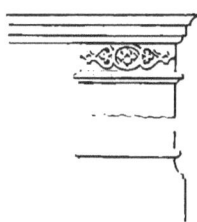

B

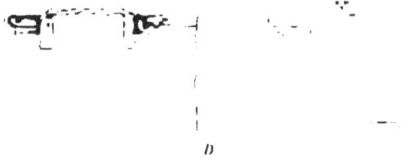

D

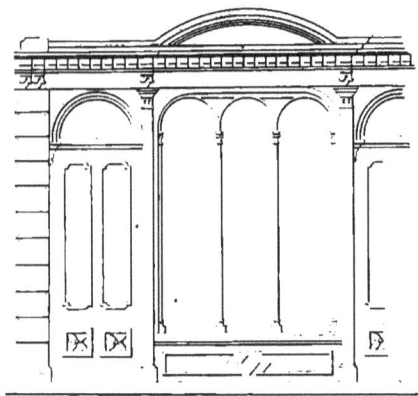

Fig. 1

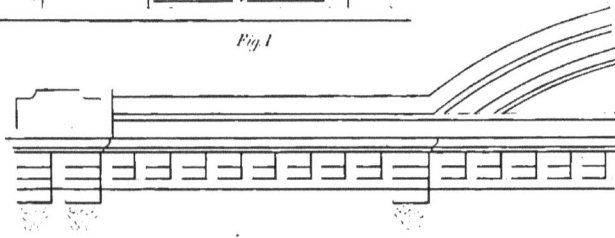

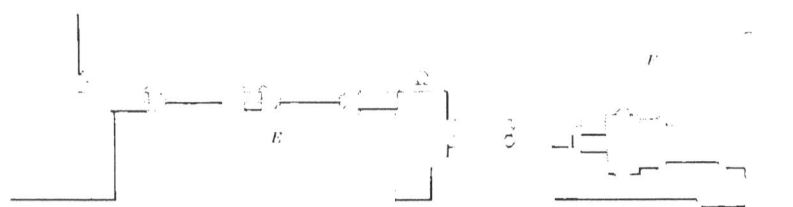

PLATE 7.

This front has end piers of stone, cut into rustic blocks having chamfered joints. The intermediate supports are of iron. The cornice may be of stone, iron, or wood; it has brackets over the piers and columns, and dentils between the brackets; in the centre of the front the cornice is formed into an arched pediment.

The window has arched lights, and small turned columns, with caps and vases, are placed in front of the sash-bars. The doors have enriched panels, and over them are moulded bars—moulded arched heads, springing from brackets, and arched headlights—and under the window are panels. A, shows a section of the cornice and upper part of the door openings; B, a section of the upper part of the window; C, an elevation of a portion of the front; D, the lower panels in the doors; E, a section of the posts, piers, doors, and window; and F, a section of the panels and sill under the window. This front should be used in a building having an elaborate exterior.

The details are drawn to a scale of ¾ of an inch to a foot.

PLATE 8.

DESIGNS FOR SHOP OR STORE FRONTS.

Figs. 1 and 2, show fronts which should be used in buildings possessing a substantial and solid appearance, and should be executed in stone. Fig. 1 has columns with caps and vases and chamfered corners. The openings are arched, and the arches are also chamfered. The cornice is simple and boldly moulded, and has plain brackets placed over the columns.

Fig. 2. Has columns fluted in front, and having caps and vases. The openings are arched at the top, and the arches have keys. The cornice consists of a few bold members, and raised and beveled panels placed in the frieze. The doors in both these designs should be hung to the stone; the columns are rebated for them. At A are the details of Fig. 1, and at B, those of Fig. 2.

The piers and posts of all store or shop fronts should rest on the foundation piers or wall, or on a stone sill course, unless the buildings are of wood.

The details are drawn to a scale of ¾ of an inch to a foot.

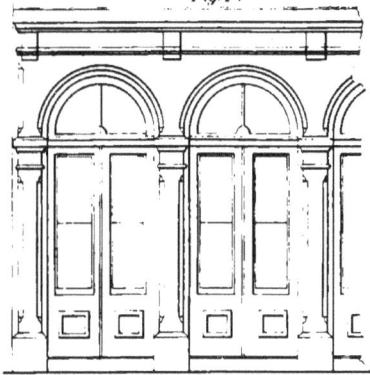

Fig. 1.

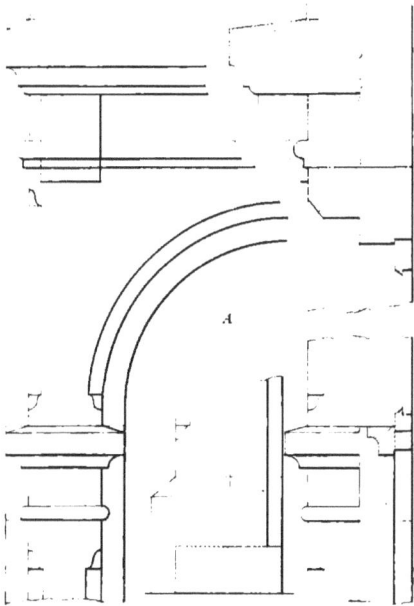

A

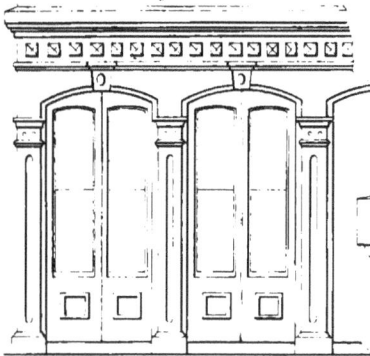

Fig. 2.

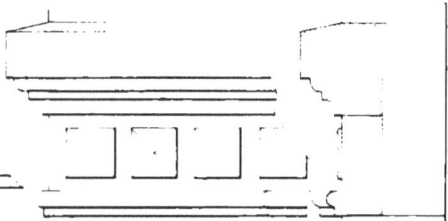

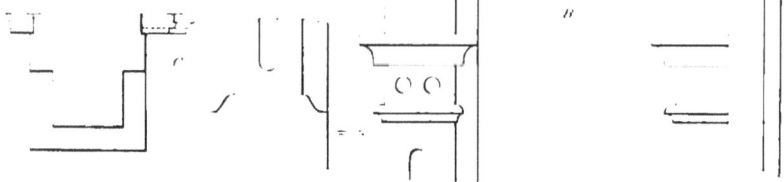

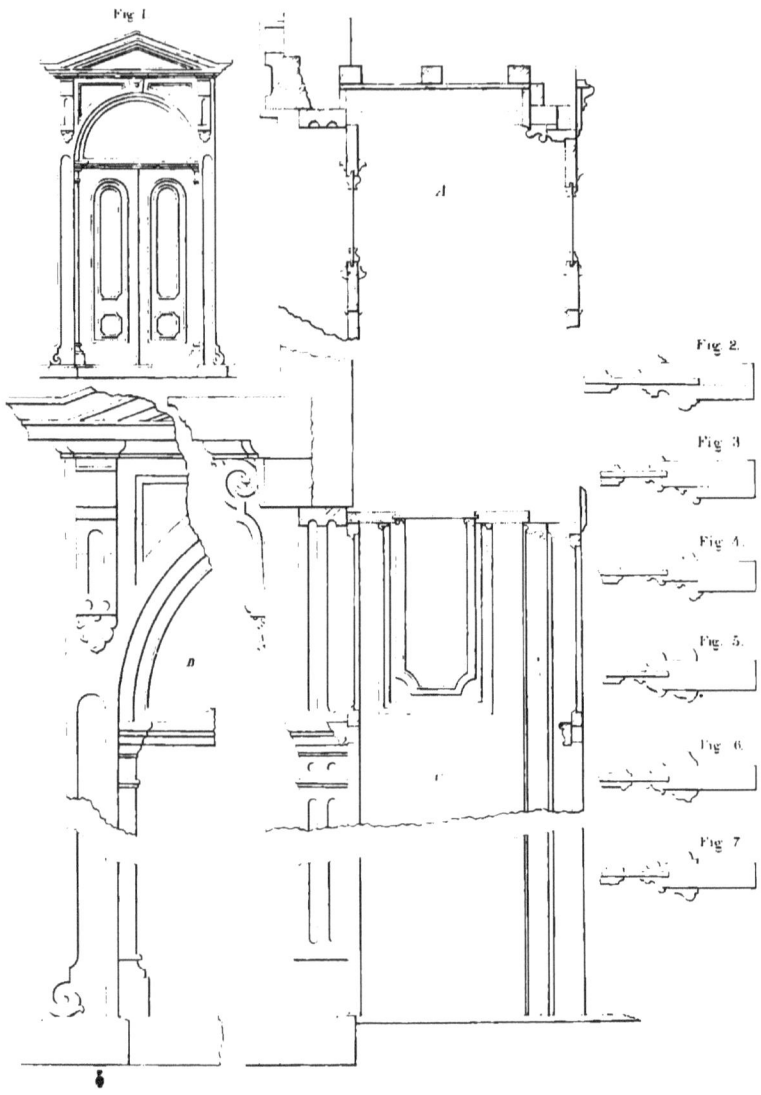

Fig 1

A

Fig 2.

Fig 3

Fig 4.

Fig 5.

Fig 6.

D

Fig 7

PLATE 9.

Fig. 1. Shows an elevation of the doors and the finish connected with them The side pilasters are moulded, and over them are carved and fluted trusses, supporting a moulded pediment cap. The headlight is arched, and the spandrils are panelled, and in the centre of the arch is a raised key.

The outside jambs of the doors are fluted, and have caps and vases : to these jambs the outer pair of doors are hung ; these doors when opened, stand at right angles to the front of the building and form the sides of the vestibule. The ceiling of the vestibule is arched and paneled the same as the doors. The inner pair of doors are made like the outer ones, and have an arched headlight and moulded jambs and finish. The exterior details of this design should be executed in stone, but they may be of wood. A, is a plan of the doors and vestibule. B, an elevation of the exterior finish. C, a section through the vestibule, showing the arched and panelled ceiling.

Figs. 2, 3, 4, 5, 6, and 7, show sections of front door stiles, panels and mouldings. Figs. 2, 3, and 4, are made of two thicknesses of plank ; the others are of one thickness, and have the outside moulding planted on the face of the doors, and this moulding should extend around both upper and lower panels, forming them into one.

The details are drawn to a scale of $\frac{3}{4}$ of an inch to the foot.

PLATE 10.

Fig. 1. Shows an entrance having moulded jambs, arched and panelled frieze, and a moulded cap, supported by enriched and fluted brackets. There are two pair of doors at the entrance, as shown in the plan at D. The doors are hung to moulded jambs, and the sides and ceiling of the vestibule are panelled. Over each pair of doors is placed a moulded bar and an arched headlight. A shows an elevation of the cap, headlight, &c. B, a profile of the cap and trusses; and C, a section of the jambs and outside doors.

Fig. 2. Shows an entrance having doors with arched headlight with enriched spandrils. The cap or hood is of heavy projection, and is supported by brackets; the frieze is panelled, and over it is a pediment surmounted by rows and gable ornament. In front of the entrance is a platform with buttresses. E shows an elevation of the cap, and F, a profile of the same.

The details are drawn to a scale of ½ inch to a foot, and the elevations of the entrances and the plan at D, to a scale of ¼ inch to a foot.

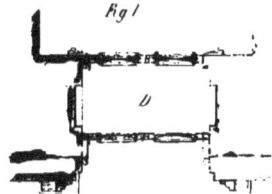

Fig 1

D

Fig 2

Fig 1

Fig 2

A

B

C

D

E

F

G

H

PLATE 11.

Fig. 1. Shows an elevation of an elaborate entrance doorway, having panelled pilasters supporting an arched and panelled frieze, and an arched pediment cap, having enriched trusses, and between them sawed dentils and a key of sawed work. The cap has a scroll at the top and the pilasters have a moulding placed in their panels, and sawed work in their caps. The outside jambs and arched soffit have raised and moulded pieces planted on their plain surface. The door jambs and their arched soffit are moulded and have a moulded outside architrave. The bar over the doors is ornamented with balls, and the headlight is arched. A shows a section of the cap and soffits; B, an elevation of the exterior details: C, an elevation of the key, and D, a section of the same; and E, an elevation and section of the scroll on top of the cap. This design may be executed in stone or wood, and should be used in a building having an elaborate front.

Fig. 2. Is a doorway having an arched cap supported by casted trusses. The jambs have small turned columns, and between these are panels formed by raised mouldings. At the bottom of the doorway, on each side, are buttress blocks which would rest on the platform of the stoop. The bar over the doors is moulded the same as the caps of the small columns of the jambs. F shows an elevation · H a section ; and G, a plan of the jambs and doors.

The details are drawn to a scale of ¾ of an inch to a foot.

PLATE 12.

Fig. 1. Shows rustic quoins applied to a front in connection with a belt course, and the cut stone work of the basement. The quoins are alternately long and short, and have chamfered joints. The string-course, or belt, is moulded, and terminates at a moulded and fluted end-block placed over the quoins. At A are the details of this design. The water-table and base-course are moulded, and in the ashlar are placed windows of a semicircular form.

Fig. 2. Has quoins of a uniform length, cut with square joints. At B are the details. Quoins may be made of equal lengths, or alternately long and short, and their joints may be chamfered square or moulded. They should always be executed in stone and placed at the corners of a building; they have a good appearance. When quoins are used, there should be belt-courses at each story of the building, placed at the floor lines.

Figs. 3, 4, and 5. Show sections and elevations of belt-courses having end-blocks which are panelled and moulded; these end-blocks should be used only when the string or belt-courses are confined to the front of the building.

Figs. 6, 7, and 8. Show designs of window-caps, with their profiles and sections.

Figs. 9 and 10. Show designs for windows having pilasters, bevelled and panelled; and pediment-caps, supported by enriched trusses. At C and D are the details. Figs. 1, 2, 9, and 10, are drawn to a scale of $\frac{1}{4}$ inch to a foot; all other drawings $\frac{7}{8}$ of an inch to a foot.

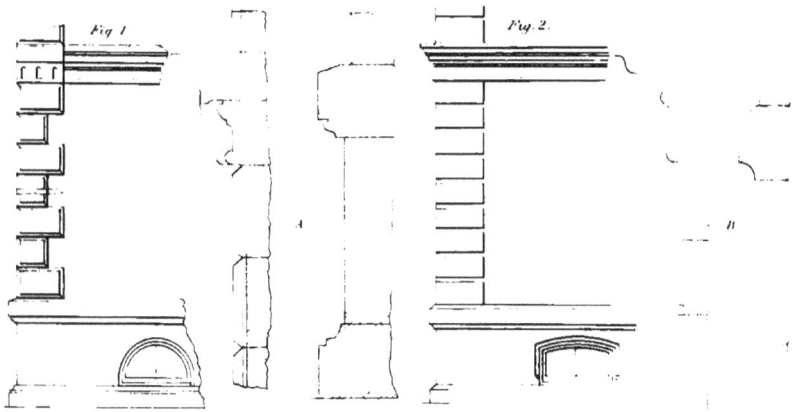

Fig 1.   Fig. 2.

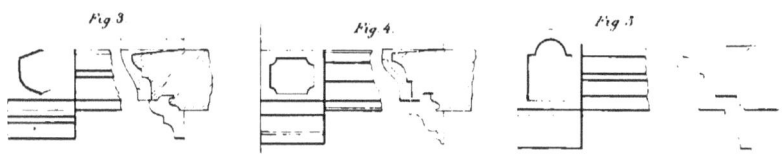

Fig 3.   Fig 4.   Fig 5.

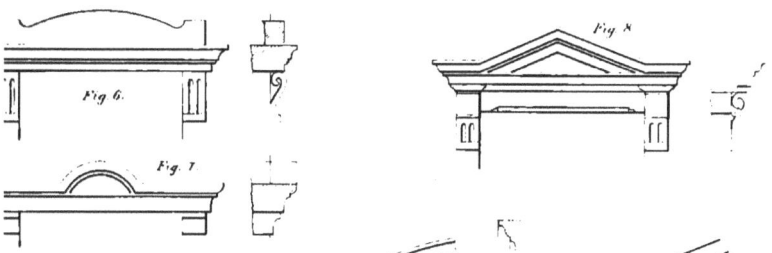

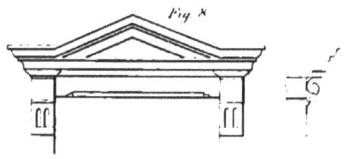

Fig 6.   Fig 8.

Fig 7.

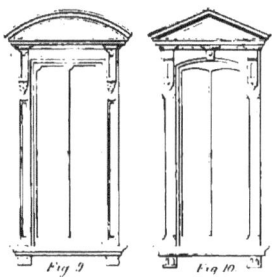

Fig 9   Fig 10.

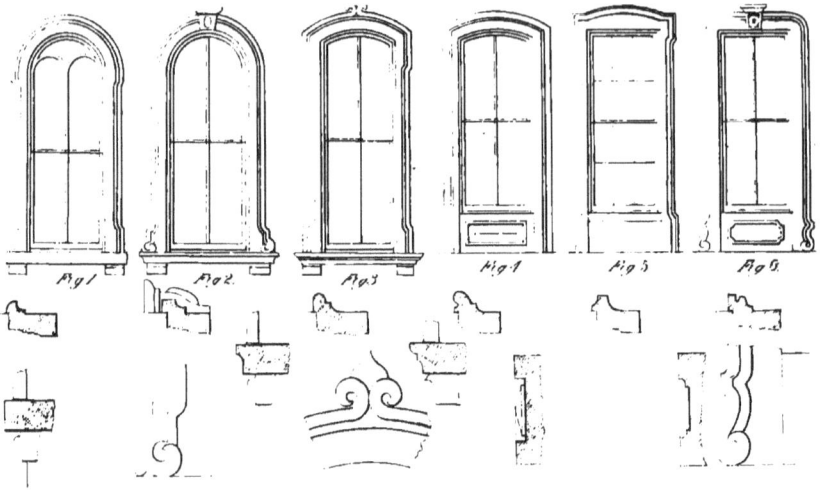

Fig 1.   Fig 2.   Fig 3.   Fig 4   Fig 5   Fig 6

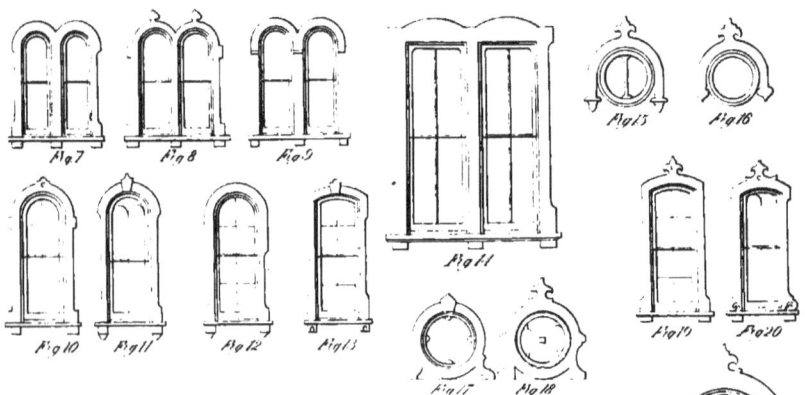

Fig 7   Fig 8   Fig 9   Fig 11   Fig 15   Fig 16

Fig 10   Fig 11   Fig 12   Fig 13   Fig 17   Fig 18   Fig 19   Fig 20

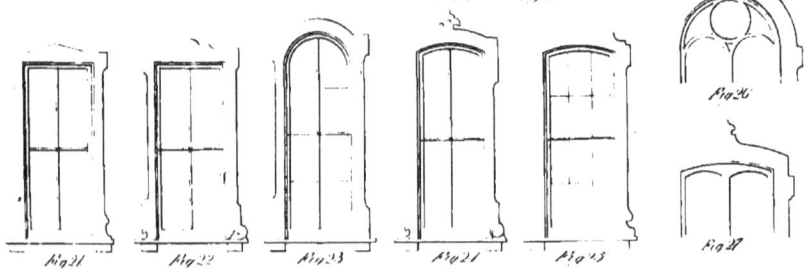

Fig 21   Fig 22   Fig 23   Fig 24   Fig 25   Fig 26   Fig 27

PLATE 13.

DESIGNS FOR THE EXTERIOR FINISH OF WINDOWS.

Figs. 1, 2, 3, 4, and 5. Show windows trimed with architraves, keys, panels, and sills. The details are shown below, and should be executed in stone. The architraves should be from 8 inches to 12 inches wide, and the sills from 5 inches to 7 inches thick. Where corbels or blocks are used under the sills, they should be placed under the architraves.

The other windows on this plate may be used in street fronts, or in suburban or country houses. The architraves should be from 1¼ inch to 2½ inches in thickness, and the sills from 2 inches to 4 inches in thickness. The small couplet windows, and those that are circular, are appropriate for gables.

Ordinary windows should be made with two, four, or twelve lights in the sash, except when they are very narrow; then they may have eight lights.

All the elevations are drawn to a scale of ¼ inch to a foot, and the details of an inch to a foot

PLATE 14.

Figs. 2, 3, 4, 5, 6, 7, 8, 9, 10, 13, 14, 15, 16, and 17. Show designs of window-caps, which may be adapted to openings of any moderate or ordinary dimensions; they may be executed in stone, iron, or wood, and are appropriate for either city or country buildings.

Fig. 12. Shows a window having moulded architraves with plain base spring and key stones. Fig. 11 shows a window having a moulded and arched head. The piers stand on a string-course, and have caps and bases. Around the window is a 4×4 inch recess in the wall, and into this the bases and caps of the piers return. A shows the cap of the piers, and B the mouldings over the windows. Figs. 9, 10, 17, and 18, are caps that should be applied to openings having architraves around them. At Fig. 1 are shown two gable windows.

The window caps may be used over doors, but when so used, they should be increased in size about one half.

All detail drawings on this plate are drawn to the scale of ¾ of an inch to the foot.

Plate 14

Fig 1

Fig 2

Fig 3

A

Fig 4

Fig 11

Fig 5

Fig 6

Fig 7

Fig 12

B

Fig 8

Fig 9

Fig 10

Fig 10

Fig 13

Fig 14

Fig 11

Fig 15

Fig 16

Fig 17

Fig 18

PLATE 15.

DESIGN OF BUILDING APPROPRIATE FOR TWO BANKING HOUSES OR INSURANCE OFFICES.

The width of the front is 40 feet. The front is intended to be entirely of stone; or the details could be of stone, and the plain wall of brick. The corner piers or quoins are 3 feet wide, rusticated as shown in detail enlarged at D. The corner quoins extend to frieze of cornice. The entrance doorway or outside doors are one step above the sidewalk, and swing back into a recessed panel; after ascending a short flight of steps, the doors to the two rooms are entered at the right or left hand. The details are drawn on the scale of $\frac{1}{4}$ an inch to a foot, and are shown by drawings A, B, C, and D.

PLATE 16.

DESIGNS FOR THREE STORES, EACH TWENTY FEET FRONT.

Drawing D represents cornice for store at the right-hand corner; also section of same. E shows cornice and pilaster-cap between 2d and 3d floors.

Drawings B and C show cornice of middle store, section, &c.; also pilaster-cap of middle store.

Drawing A shows cornice of corner store at the left, and section of cornice.

These stores are drawn with the intention of making the main part of the front brick, and the details of cut stone. The smaller columns for the corner stores to be of iron. The cornices are designed to be made of wood.

Fig 1.

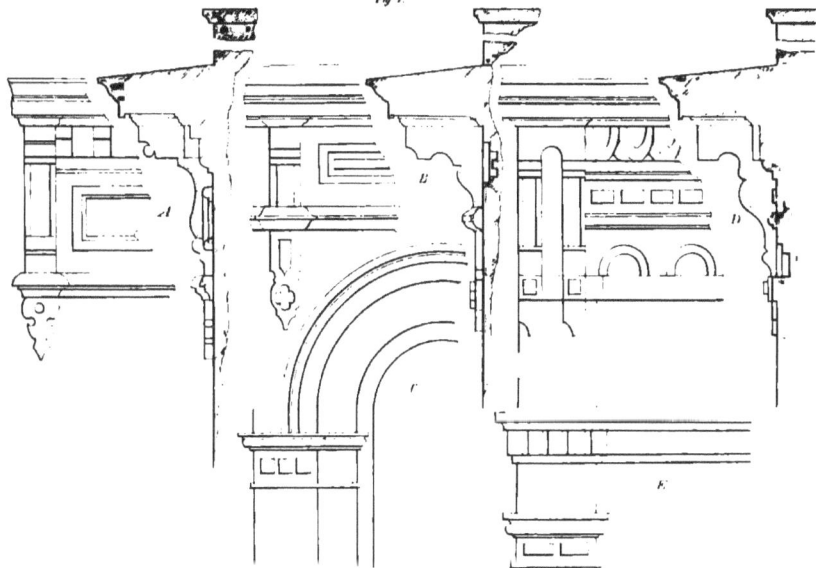

.

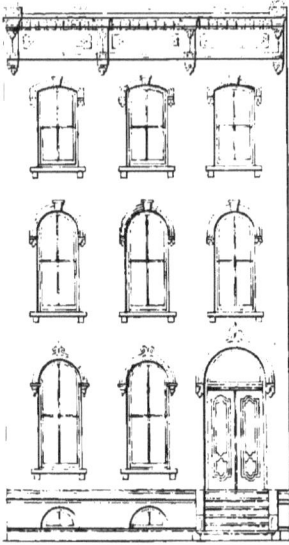

Fig. 1.

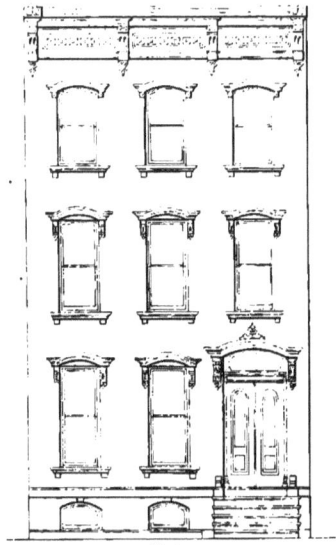

Fig. 2.

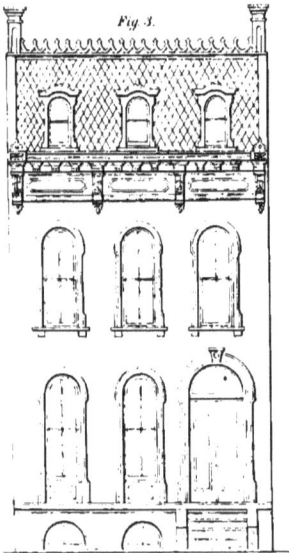

Fig. 3.

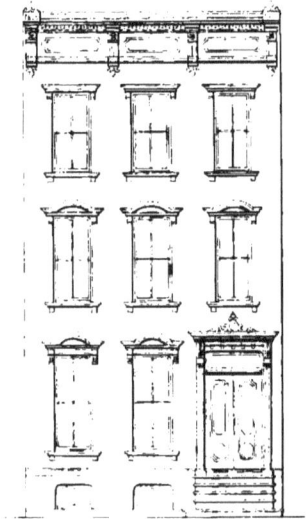

Fig. 4.

PLATE 17.

This Plate shows four designs for street fronts of dwelling-houses, each three stories in height. The water-table, ashlar, and base-course in each design should be of cut stone. The walls may be of stone or brick, and the sills and caps of the windows and doors of stone, cast-iron, or wood; if of wood, the caps should be covered with tin on the top. The cornices are designed to be constructed of wood, but they may be of stone or galvanized sheet-iron.

The cornice of Fig. 1 is shown at Fig. 1 on Plate 1; the caps of the windows and the door, at Figs. 13 and 14, on Plate 14. The cut-stone work of basement is shown on Plate 12, at Fig. 1. The cornice of Fig. 2 is shown at Fig. 2, Plate 1; the window-caps at Fig. 16, Plate 14, and Plate 38, Fig. 5. The entrance-doors with their finish are shown at Fig. 2, Plate 11.

The cornice of Fig. 3 is shown at Fig. 1, Plate 2; the window-caps at Figs. 1 and 4, Plate 13; and the entrance-doors at Fig. 1, Plate 13.

The cornice of Fig. 4 is shown at Fig. 2, Plate 2; the window-caps at Figs. 2 and 4, Plate 1; and the entrance-doors at Fig. 1, Plate 38.

Fig. 3 has a curved roof, which should be covered with slate; in the roof are dormer windows which light the third story. At the top of the curve is a light cornice and a railing, which should be of iron.

PLATE 18.

Fig. 1. Shows a two-story building designed for a store. The front should be of brick. The cornice is shown at Fig. 1, Plate 25; the window-caps at Fig. 4, Plate 1.

Fig. 2. Shows a three-story building designed for a retail store. The front may be of stone or brick. The cornice is shown at Fig. 2, Plate 1; the window-caps at Fig. 19, Plate 14; and the front of first story at Fig. 1, Plate 17.

Fig. 3. Shows a front of a dwelling-house, of an elaborate character. This front should be executed in stone. The cornice is shown at Fig. 2, Plate 3; the windows at Figs. 9 and 10, Plate 12; the front entrance-doors and their finish at Fig. 1, Plate 11; and the quoins, belt-courses, and work of basement, at Fig. 1, Plate 12.

Fig. 4. Shows a front of a dwelling, which is quite plain in its details. The wall should be of brick, and the basement of stone. The cornice is shown at Fig. 3, Plate 1, and the window and door-caps at Fig. 4, Plate 1

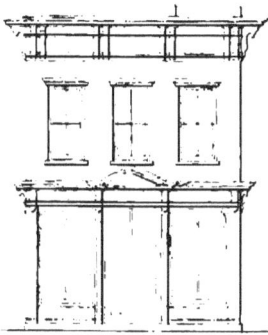

Fig. 1

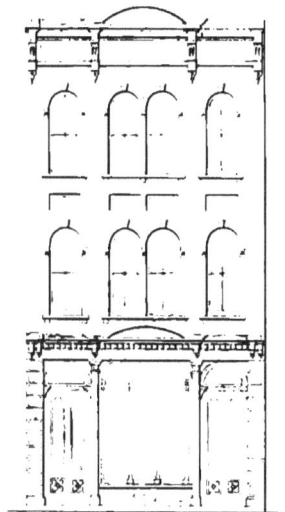

Fig. 2

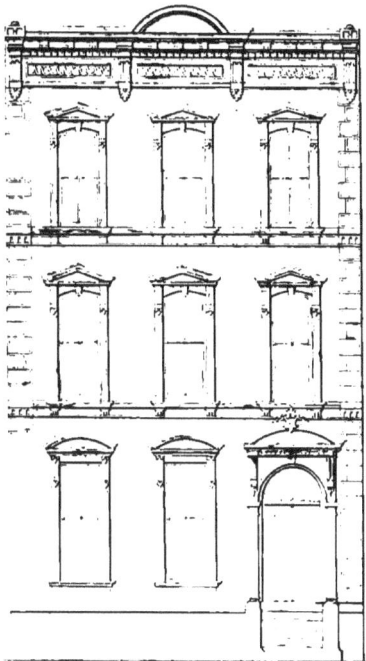

Fig. 3

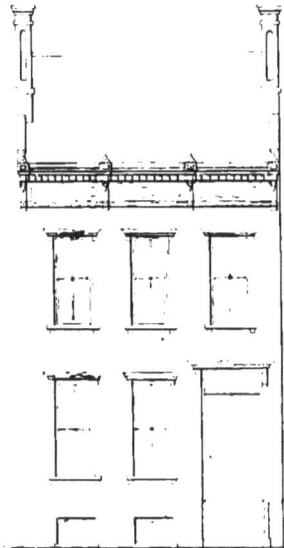

Fig. 4

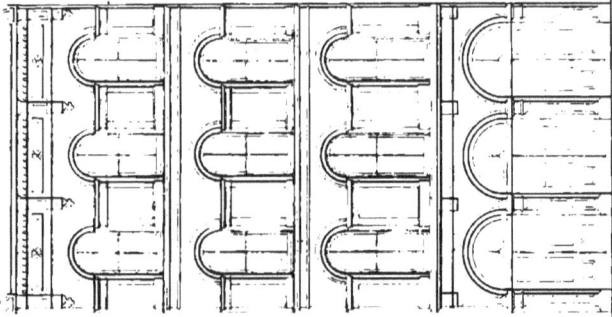

Fig. 3.

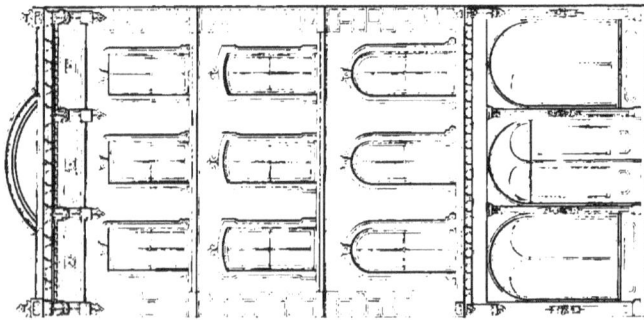

Fig. 2.

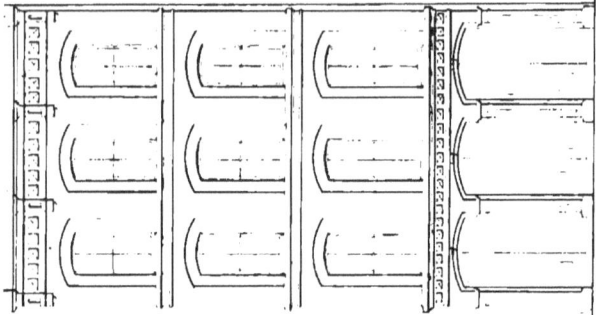

Fig. 1.

PLATE 19.

ELEVATIONS OF STREET FRONTS FOR STORES.

Fig. 1. Shows a design for a store. The front of first story should be of stone, also the belt-courses under the windows of the 3d and 4th stories. The front of the building above the 1st story should be of brick; the windows have recesses around them 4 inches deep. The cornice is shown at Fig. 1, Plate 24, and the front of 1st story at Fig. 2, Plate 8.

Fig. 2. Shows a front which should be of stone above the 1st story. The cornice is shown at Fig. 1, Plate 3; the belt-courses at Fig. 4, Plate 12; the quoins at Fig. 1, Plate 12; and the windows at Figs. 5, 2, and 3, Plate 13. The front of 1st story is shown at Fig. 2, Plate 10.

Fig. 3. Shows a front which should be of cut stone, or the front above the 1st story may be of brick, with cast-iron dressings. The cornice is shown at Fig. 2, Plate 24; the windows and dressings of the piers at Fig. 11, Plate 14; and the 1st story front, at Fig. 1, Plate 8.

Figs. 1 and 3 are designed for wholesale stores, and Fig. 2 is designed for a retail store. These fronts are drawn of an inch to a foot.

PLATE 20.

Fig. 1 A part of design for a four-story front, with Doric entablature for 1st story and arcade. All of the details are intended to be of stone, including the columns of 1st story, cornice of 1st story, corner pilaster, arcade, &c. The quoins are to be of stone, cut with bevel joint. The window-caps and architraves of window-caps are also of stone. The main cornice is intended to be of stone, with sunk panels between carved brackets. The balustrade can be left off if desirable. This design is intended for an expensive stone front; if the cornices cannot be returned as drawn in the design, they can be constructed so as to butt into blocks at the corner, as shown in cornices on Plate 1, Fig. A or B.

Fig. 2. Design for street front with one door at the side, for entrances to offices above; the door at the other side as entrance to store. The corner piers and columns of the 1st story can be made of stone or iron; also the arches can be either stone or iron. The pilasters running up at the sides to the cornice are 2 feet wide, cut with bead on each angle. The windows are all circular head, with pilaster-caps at the spring of arch, and a plain stone arch. The string-courses are all intended to be of stone; also columns of 5th story, and main cornice of the building.

These designs are drawn on the scale of $\frac{1}{8}$ of an inch to a foot.

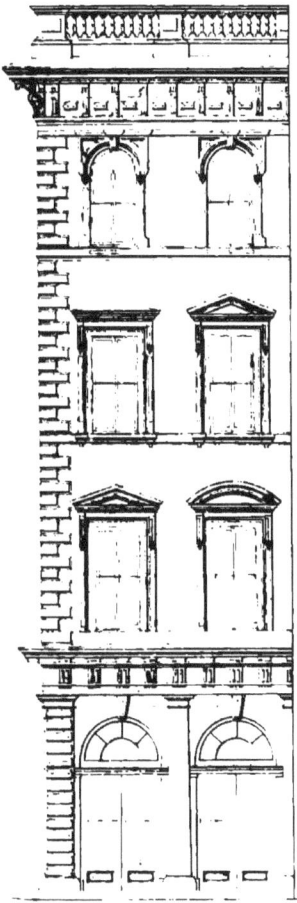

Fig 1   Fig 2

Plate 21.

Plate 23

PLATES 21, 22, AND 23,

Are designs intended for first-class street architecture, and the fronts built entirely of stone. They are well adapted for designs of fronts for banking-houses. The fronts of each building are 50 feet. Plate 21 shows a design with three openings in the front. Plate 23, designed for five openings in the front. The lower part or first story of both of the fronts is drawn with the Doric entablature. The cornice of Plate 23 is a cornice with brackets or cantilevers. The cornice of Plate 21 is a design for a modillion cornice with dentils; each designed to be made of stone.

The Plates are drawn on the scale of ' of an inch to a foot.

Plate 22. Design for Gothic front of 40 feet; with design of Bank on one side and store on the other. The 2d story designed for offices. The 3d story designed for public hall. The entire front should be built of stone.

PLATE 24.

Figs. 1 and 2. Show plain cornices, boldly moulded, and having fluted and chamfered trusses, and raised and bevelled panels in the frieze; these cornices are designed for street fronts.

Fig. 4. Shows a cornice designed for street fronts, having moulded and enriched brackets, which should be placed 3½ feet from centres; the frieze between them is panelled.

Figs. 3 and 8. Show cornices having sawed modillions, 6 inches thick, placed 16 inches apart.

Figs. 6, 7, and 5, are cornices designed for country houses of moderate dimensions.

Fig. 5 has brackets resting on the string-moulding, and between them are sawed dentils.

Fig. 6 has a sawed verge-board 2 inches thick, and no brackets.

Fig. 7 has raised panels nailed to the frieze-board.

All details on this Plate are ¾ of an inch to a foot.

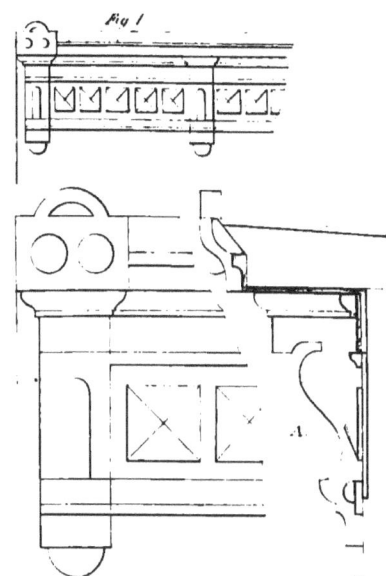

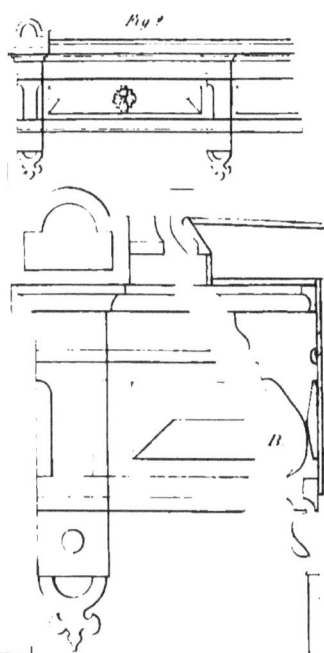

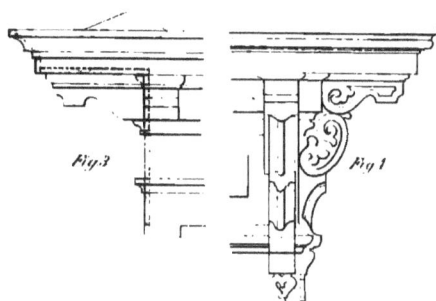

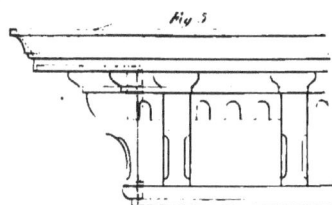

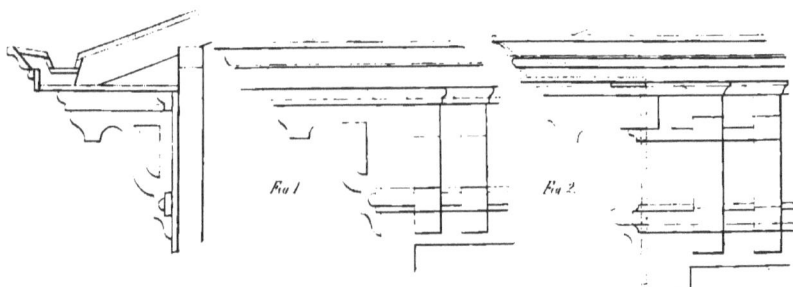

Fig 1. Fig 2.

Fig 3 Fig 4.

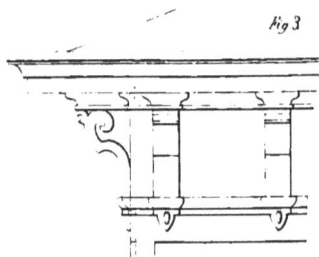
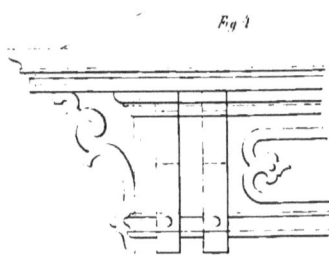

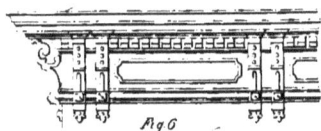
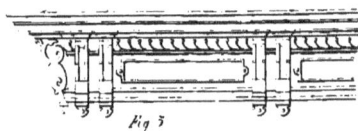

Fig 6. Fig 5.

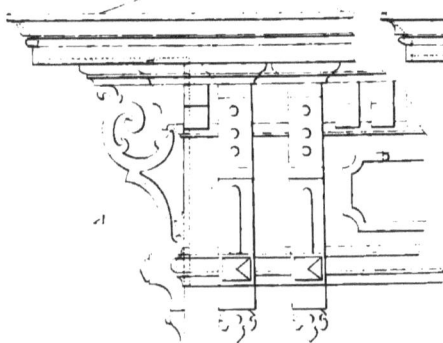
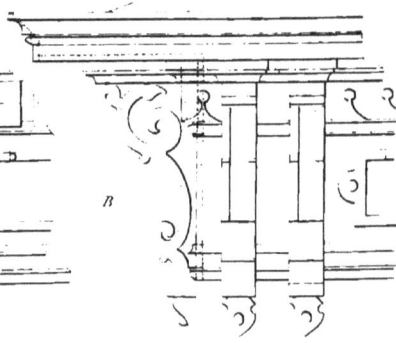

A B

PLATE 25.

Fig. 1. Design of cornice for two-story cottage. Whole height of cornice, 2 feet 8 inches. Projection of cornice, 2 feet 4 inches. The thickness of brackets 4 inches, and placed in pairs 4 inches apart.

Fig. 2. Design of cornice for two-story suburban residence. Projection of cornice, 2 feet 1 inch, and the whole height about 3 feet. The brackets are 5 inches thick, and placed in pairs 5 inches apart; in this cornice are dentils 3½ inches wide by 4½ inches high, placed about 2 inches apart.

Fig. 3. Design of cornice for cottage. Projection of cornice, 1 foot 10 inches; height, 2 feet 3 inches. The brackets are 4 inches thick, and placed about 1 foot 7 inches apart from centres.

Fig. 4. Design of cornice, 1 foot 10 inches; projection—height, 2 feet 8 inches. Brackets 4 inches thick, placed in pairs. The panels between the brackets are ornamented by a strip 1½ 2 inches forming a raised panel with ornamental ends as shown in design.

Figs 5 and 6. Designs of two good cornices for villas. Projection of cornice. Fig. 5, to be 2 feet 6 inches; cornice Fig. 6, projection 2 feet 8 inches—height of both cornices about 4 feet. The brackets of both are 6 inches thick, placed in pairs 6 inches apart. The designs of both are about the same size: the variations are made in the different moulded crown-mould, bed-mould, dentils—ornamental panel—profile of bracket—frieze string-course, &c., as can be readily understood by referring to enlarged drawings of cornices of Figs. 5 and 6, at A and B. All of the cornices on this Plate are drawn on the scale of ⅞ of an inch to a foot, except Figs. 5 and 6, which are ½ of an inch to a foot.

PLATE 26.

Figs. 1, 2, 3, 4, 6, 7, 8, 9, 10, 11, and 14 are drawn to the scale of ¼ an inch to a foot. Figs. 5, 12, 13, 15, 16, and 17, are drawn to the scale of ⅜ of an inch to a foot.

Fig. 1. Design of plain Italian cornice, 1 foot projection, 1 foot 9 inches high

Fig. 2. Similar design, 1 foot 3 inches projection, 2 feet 2 inches high.

Fig. 3. Design of dentil cornice, 2 feet projection, and 4 feet 6 inches high.

Fig. 4. Design of modillion cornice, 2 feet projection, and 4 feet 6 inches high.

Fig. 5. Design for cottage cornice, for gable-ends, 1 foot 6 inches projection height 2 feet 4 inches.

Fig. 6. Design of block cornice 1 foot 6 inches projection, and 2 feet 3 inches high

Fig. 7. Block cornice 2 feet projection, 2 feet 2 inches high.

Fig. 8. Modillion cornice with carved modillion. Projection of cornice 2 feet, height 2 feet 1 inch.

Fig. 9. Cantilever cornice with carved modillion and ornamental truss or cantilever. Projection of cornice 2 feet; height 3 feet 5 inches, not including ornamental pattern under each bracket. The brackets of this cornice should be placed about 2 feet apart from centres, so as to make the sunk panels between brackets a square.

Fig. 10. Similar cornice to the one above described, with 2 feet 6 inches projection; height 5 feet 1 inch. Brackets are 7 inches thick, and placed apart a sufficient distance to make the sunk panel a square. This cornice is a very appropriate and suitable cornice for street architecture.

Fig. 11. Cornice 2 feet 6 inches projection; height 5 feet 1 inch, with plain modillion and cantilever.

Fig. 12. Cottage or villa cornice, with 1 foot 6 inches projection. Block modillions 4 inches square, placed about 14 inches apart from centres.

Fig. 13. Villa cornice with 2 feet 7 inches projection, 3 feet high. Brackets 5 inches thick, placed in pairs 5 inches apart. The panels between pairs are made by 1½ inch piece fillet and cove, as shown in drawing.

Fig. 14. Design of large cornice with 3 feet projection and 5 feet 10 inches high. The brackets are 9 inches thick, placed in pairs 1 foot 1 inch apart. The panels between the brackets are sunk. For sizes and dimensions of details, measure on the scale of half an inch to a foot.

Fig. 15. Design of horizontal cornice for villa or cottage, projection 1 foot 10 inches; height 2 feet 6 inches. The brackets are 4 inches thick, placed 16 inches apart from centres.

Fig. 16. Cornice similar to the one above described, with 1 foot 9 inches projection; 2 feet 4 inches high. No brackets on this, but finished with heavy bed-mould and ornamental dentils.

Fig. 17. Cottage or villa cornice, with ornamental bracket 4 inches thick; projection 1 foot 10 inches.

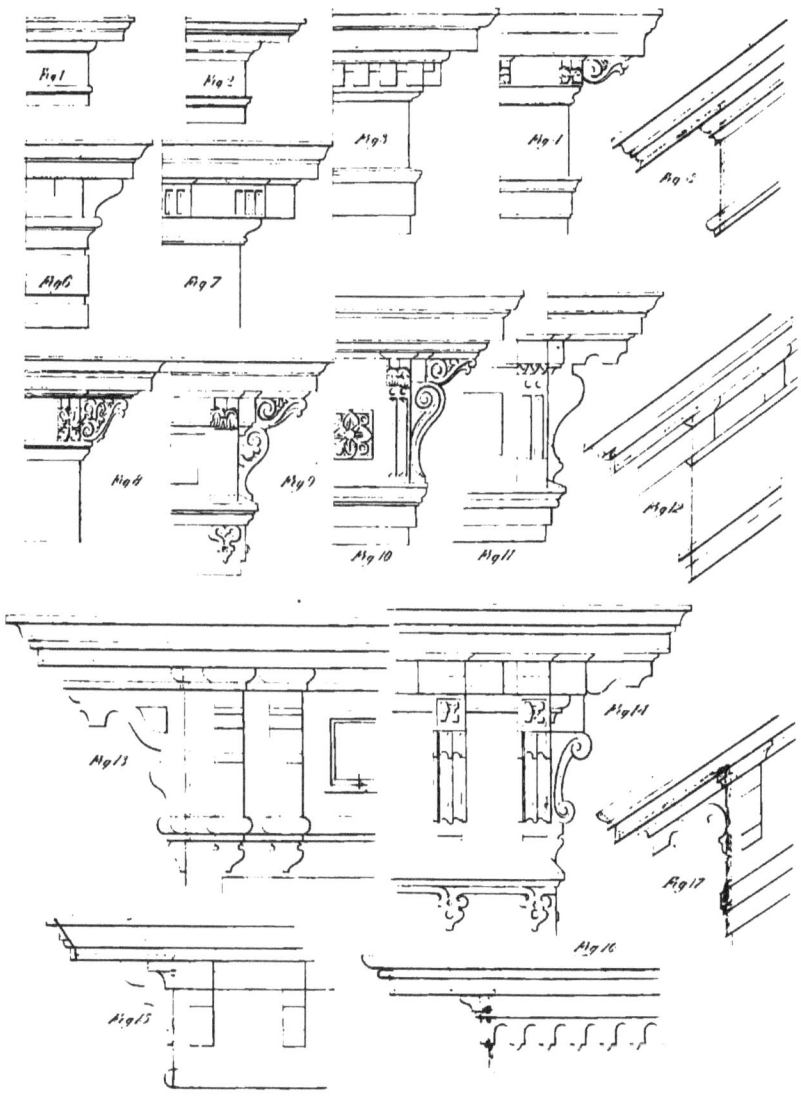

Fig 1. Fig 2. Fig 3. Fig 4. Fig 5.
Fig 6. Fig 7.
Fig 8. Fig 9. Fig 10. Fig 11. Fig 12.
Fig 13. Fig 14. Fig 17.
Fig 15. Fig 16.

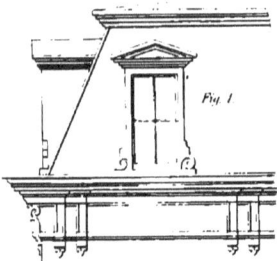

Fig 1.

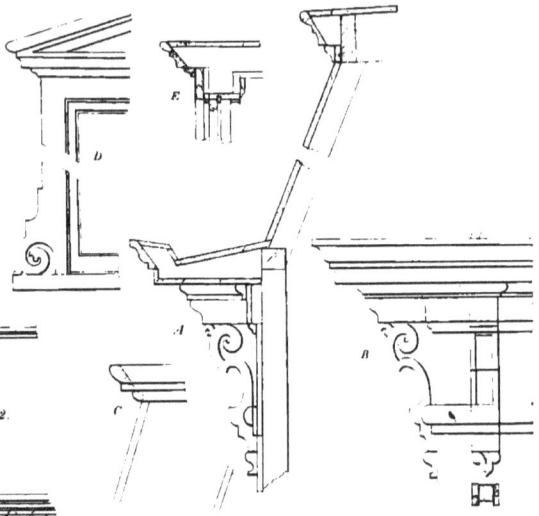

Fig 2.

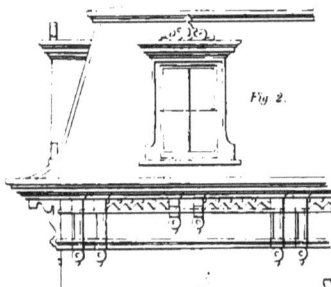

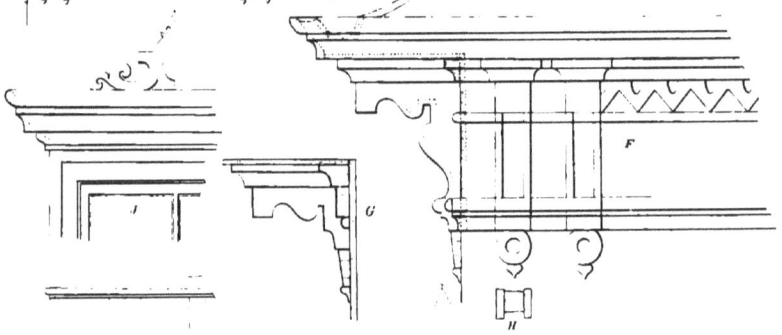

PLATE 27.

DESIGNS FOR CORNICES, CURVED OR FRENCH ROOFS, AND DORMER WINDOWS.

Fig. 1. Shows a roof with straight rafters. The cornice has scroll-sawed brackets with moulded caps The dormer windows have sawed plank casings, and moulded pediment-caps. At the top of the steep roof is a light cornice. A shows a section of the cornices and roof; B, an elevation of the main cornice : D, an elevation of the dormer window ; and E. a section of its cornice.

Fig. 2. Shows a roof, curved at the foot. The main cornice has sawed brackets placed in pairs, and between them are smaller brackets and sawed dentils. The dormer window has a moulded cap and scroll. F shows the main cornice : G. a section of the small brackets and sawed dentils ; H, a section of the main brackets : and I. the dormer window-cap and scroll.

Fig. 3. Shows a roof curved at the foot. The cornice has sawed brackets, resting on the string or architrave moulding. K shows the cornice, and L, the moulding at the top of the roof.

Details, $\frac{3}{4}$ of an inch to a foot. Designs are drawn $\frac{1}{4}$ of an inch to a foot.

PLATE 28.

Fig. 1. Has a cornice with moulded and enriched trusses, and between the trusses the frieze is plain, and over the frieze are plain modillions; and moulded modillions are placed over the trusses. The roof is curved, and at the top of the curve is a moulded cornice, and over this, on the flat portion of the roof, is a balustrade having panelled pedestals, surmounted by turned urns. The balusters in the railing are turned. The dormer windows have panelled pilasters and arched pediment-cap, supported by sawed and fluted trusses with sawed leaves. At the bottom of the dormer windows, on each side, are sawed and fluted trusses, resting on the sill. A shows an elevation of the dormer window, and B, a section of the same. C shows an elevation of the upper cornice and railing, and D, a section of the same. E shows a detail of the main cornice; F, the modillions; G, a side-view of the lower trusses of the dormer window; and H, a section of the front of the trusses of main cornice.

Figs. 4, 2, and 3, show cornices and balustrades suitable for the top of curved roofs. Fig. 2 has pedestals and balustrade of 2 inches plank; Fig. 3 has plank balustrade; and Fig. 4 has panelled pedestals with turned urns. The railing has moulded cap and base, and sawed open-work.

The details of this Plate are drawn on the scale of ¾ of an inch to a foot. The designs are drawn on the scale of ¼ of an inch to a foot.

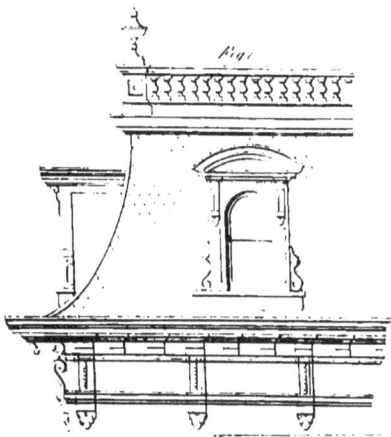

Fig.1

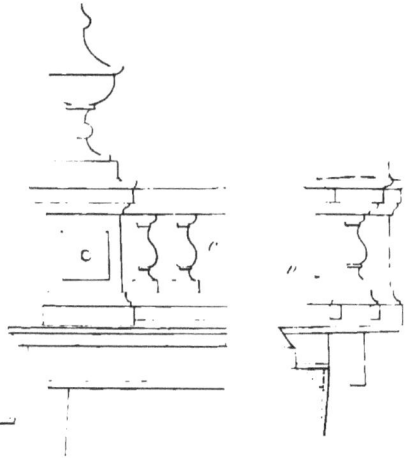

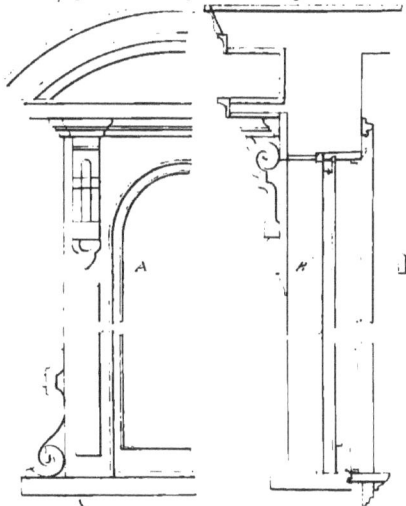

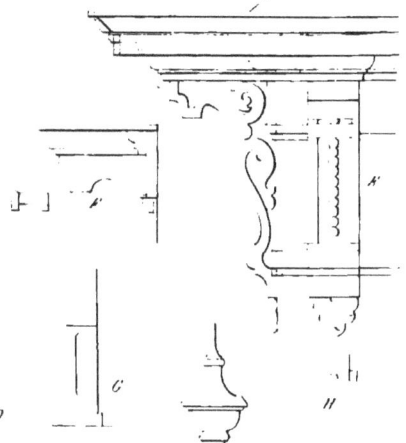

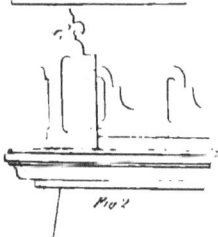

Fig.2

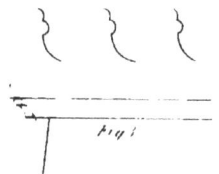

Fig.1

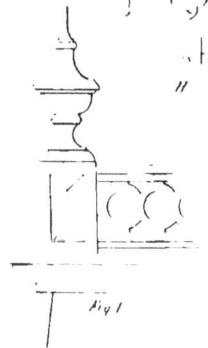

Fig.1

PLATE 29.

Designs A and B. Are intended for Gothic gables, springing-stones, and cornice. Drawings at A, represent the face and side-view of springing-stone, and moulded coping; also the manner of butting the cornice into springing-stones. B, shows the gable-point or apex of gable, and trefoil beads or mouldings at the point of roof.

Design C. Shows ornamental gable; the ornaments or tracery are intended to be cut out of 2-inch plank; also the ornament at eaves of gable roof. The finial post is 6 inches square. The top or finale made of 4 pieces of 2-inch plank, put together as per pattern, with side pieces running down gable, butting into finial post.

Design D. Represents cornice with coved bed-mould and finial at top of 2-inch plank. The projection of cornice is 2 feet.

Design E. Shows ornamental verge-board. The verge-board is intended to be cut out of 1½-inch plank. The finial to be cut out of 2-inch plank. The projection of cornice is 2 feet.

Design F. Is ornamental gable with steep roof. The verge-board to be cut out of 2-inch plank. G, shows finial of same gable.

Design H. Shows ornamental gable; the verge-board to be cut out of 1½-inch stuff. The finial to be 6 inches square. The top or finale to be made of 4 pieces of 2-inch plank, put together as shown in drawing, with carved top. The bottom of finial to be moulded; upper moulding square, others beneath turned.

Designs I and K. Are designs for finials for roofs. These are 8 inches square above apex of roof, and covered as shown in designs.

All of the designs on this plate are drawn on the scale of ½ an inch to the foot.

PLATE 30.

Fig. 1. Design for ornamented gable. Post 5×5 for finial; cross-piece made of 3-inch stuff; the filling-in ornament of 1½-inch stuff. For design enlarged see drawings A and B. (See Plate 52, Fig. 4, Gable in Cottage.)

Fig. 2. Ornamental gable. Verge-board made of 1½-inch plank. Finial 5 inches square. D shows section of cornice on the rake of gable.

Fig. 3. Ornamental gable. Verge-board made of 1½-inch plank. C shows section of cornice on the rake.

Figs. 4 and 5. Drawings of ornamental constructed gable designs. The braces are made of 3-inch plank, bevelled on the edges. The cross-bar of Fig. 4 should be 6×6 inches. See Plate 52, Fig. 3, for the gable in design of cottage.

Designs 6, 7, 8, and 9. Are finial designs for gables, made of 2-inch plank.

Figs. 10, 11, and 12. Are sawed ornaments or finials, for window-caps, &c.

Fig. 13. Shows front and side of plain chimney-top, base, &c.

All these designs are drawn on the scale of ¾ of an inch to a foot, except Figs. 1, 4, 5, and 13; the latter are drawn on the scale of ½ of an inch to a foot.

Plate 30

A

Fig 1

D

Fig. 2

B

Fig 3

C

Fig. 6.

Fig. 12

Fig. 4

Fig. 5

Fig. 14

Fig. 10

Fig. 7

Fig. 9

Fig. 8

Fig 8

Fig 9

Fig 10

Fig 11

Fig 12

Fig 13

Fig 1

Fig 2

Fig 3

Fig 4

Fig 5

Fig 6

Fig 7

PLATE 31.

DESIGNS FOR WINDOW-CAPS.

Figs. 1, 2, 3, 4, 5, 6, and 7. Show caps, designed to be constructed of wood The brackets supporting the caps are to be sawed from plank, and the enrichments to be of sawed or carved work. The scrolls on the caps should be 3 inches thick, and the caps may be used on windows, with or without architraves. Figs. 8 and 9, show arched caps, which should be made of stone or iron. The keys and corbels are enriched.

Figs. 10 and 11. Show caps or hoods, suitable for cheap cottages, and are made of 3-inch plank, supported by sawed blocks.

Figs. 12 and 13. Show moulded caps, supported by carved trusses; they should be used on openings having moulded architraves.

The designs on this plate are drawn to a scale of ¾ of an inch to the foot.

PLATE 32.

Fig. 1. Has columns of 2-inch plank, with openings cut through them. The cornice has plain modillions, and a plain arched frieze 2 inches thick. The balustrade is of 2-inch plank. At A are the details.

Fig. 2. Has coupled columns and between them an arched frieze 3 inches thick. The roof over the cornice is arched, and at the top of the curved portion is a sawed balustrade. C shows the details of the cornice and columns, and E the balustrade.

Fig. 3. Has square columns with wide fluting in the centre. The frieze is arched, and has plain sawed brackets. The balustrade is of 1½-inch plank. with a scroll in the centre. At D are the details.

Fig. 4. Has square fluted columns with carved capitals and panelled pedestals. The frieze is arched and moulded. The cornice has sawed modillions, with leaves. The balustrade is sawed from 3-inch plank. At E and F are the details.

Fig. 5. Has plank columns, with fluted capitals and moulded bases. The cornice has small sawed blocks placed over the columns. The balustrade is of sawed plank. H shows the details of the cornice and columns, and G, those of the balustrade.

Fig. 6. Shows a design for a door-cap supported by scroll sawed brackets.

The designs are ¼ inch to the foot; and the details ⅜ of an inch to the foot. I shows a design for an urn.

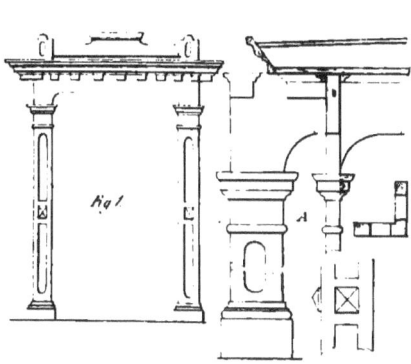

Fig 1.

A

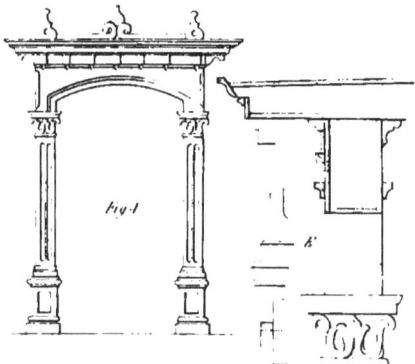

Fig 1.

E

F

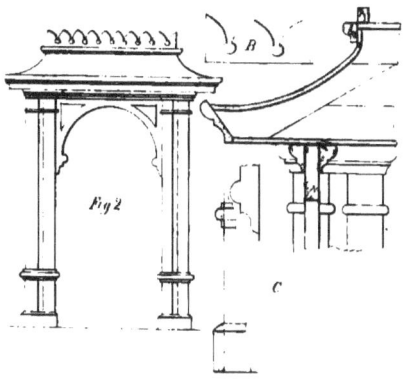

Fig 2.

B

C

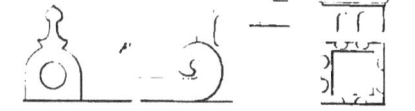

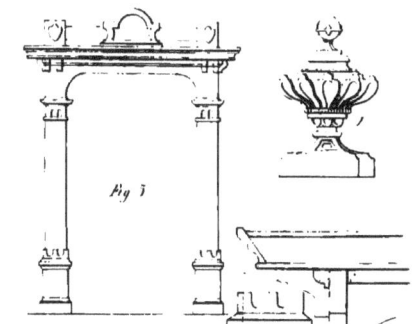

Fig 3.

I

G

H

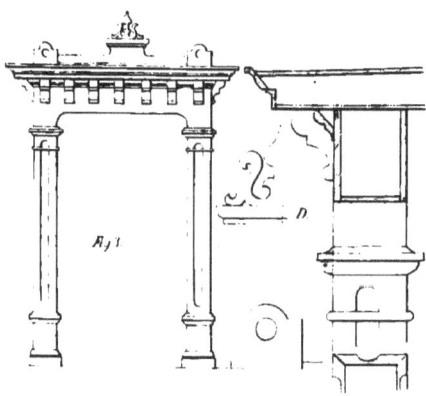

Fig 1.

D

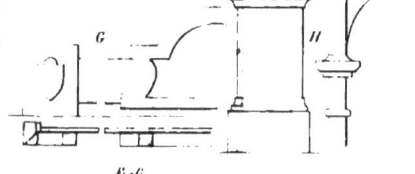

Fig 6.

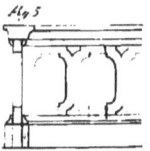

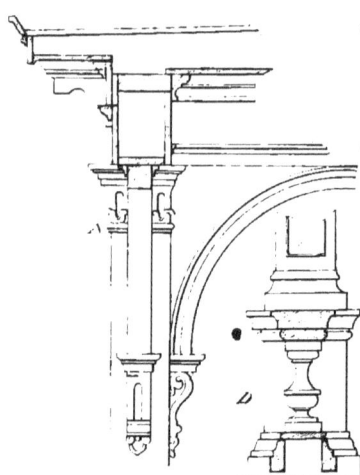

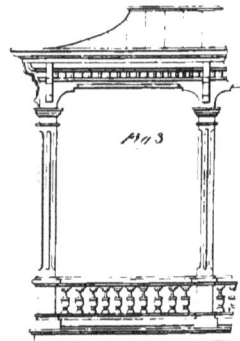

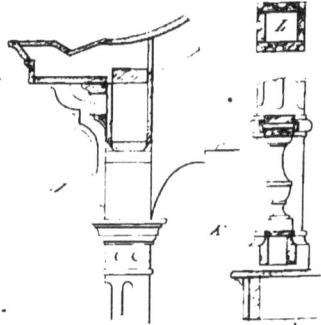

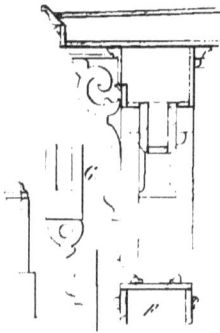

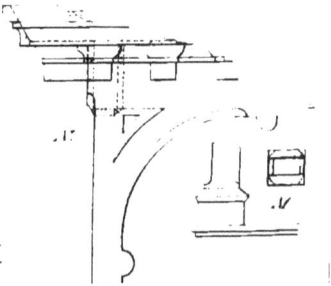

PLATE 33.

DESIGNS FOR PORCHES.

Fig. 1. Has columns 10 inches square, having panelled shafts, carved capitals and moulded bases. The pedestals of the columns are panelled, and have moulded top and bases. The railing between the pedestals has turned balusters. The cornice has modillions 5 inches thick, with sawed leaves. Between the columns are moulded arches, resting on sawed and fluted trusses. The railing on the roof has moulded cap and base, turned balusters, and panelled pedestals. A shows a section of the cornice and arches, and the capitals of the columns; B, a section of the columns; C, a section of the railing of the roof; and E, a section of the pedestals of the columns. This piazza should be used in a large dwelling of elaborate design.

Fig. 2. Has square panelled columns, arched frieze with dentils, and the cornice has sawed trusses. The balustrade consists of end and centre scrolls, 3 inches thick. G shows the details of the cornice; F, a section of the columns; and H, the scrolls on the roof.

Fig. 3. Has columns 8 inches square, chamfered on the corners, and fluted on the sides. The capitals and bases are moulded. The railing has moulded cap and base, and turned balusters. The cornice has a frieze, arched from the columns, and chamfered on the level portion of the soffit. The brackets are 3 inches thick, and between them are plain dentils. The roof is curved, and has a bold moulding at the top. J shows the capital of the columns and the cornice; K, a section of the railing; and L, a section of the columns.

Fig. 4. Has columns 6 inches square, with chamfered corners. The arches and frieze are 6 inches thick and are chamfered. The cornice has plain modillions. At M and N are the details.

The designs are ¼ inch to a foot, and the details ¾ of an inch to the foot.

PLATE 34.

Fig. 1. Design for Gothic veranda ; columns 6 inches in diameter—round, with turned cap and base. Balustrade made of 2-inch plank, cut with Gothic arches, coved with crisps, and cut through. The brackets over each column are 6 inches thick ; intermediate brackets are 4 inches thick. Lower balustrade to be made of 2-inch plank. Lower balustrade is 2 feet 3 inches high. Upper balustrade 2 feet high. Projection of cornice to be 16 inches. For a more distinct view of details of veranda Fig. 1, see drawing A, which is on the scale of ¼ an inch to a foot.

Fig. 2. Design of Gothic veranda. The columns or supports are 12 inches wide, 4 inches thick, panelled, and moulded, as shown in drawing B, of section through corner support or column. The tracery in angle to be made of 2-inch plank. Upper and lower balustrade filling-in to be of 2-inch plank. Lower balustrade to be 2 feet 1 inch high ; upper balustrade to be 2 feet high. For enlarged drawing of veranda details, see drawing B.

Fig. 3. Design for window-cap.

Drawings C, D, E, F, and G. Designs of vases for tops of balustrades for cornices of street architecture, or finish of pedestals to any cornice. These vases are drawn on the scale of ¾ of an inch to a foot.

Figs. 1 and 2 are drawn on the scale of ¼ of an inch to a foot ; A and B on the scale of ½ an inch to a foot.

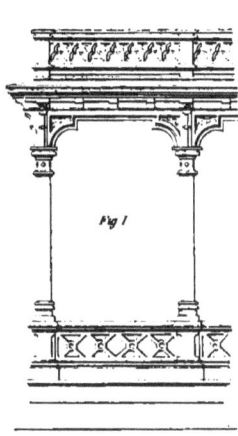

Fig 1

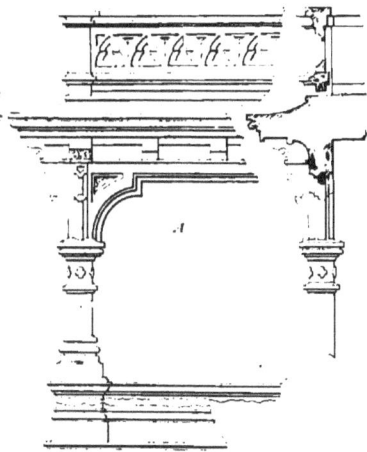

A

G

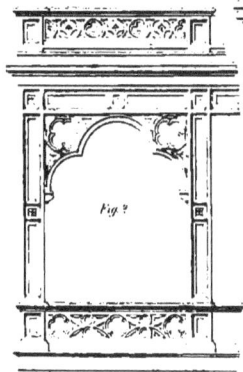

Fig 2

B

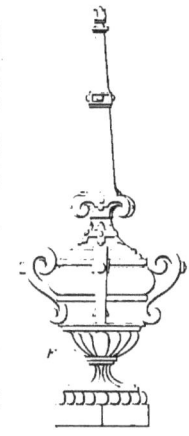

F

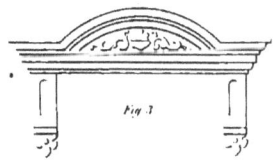

Fig 3

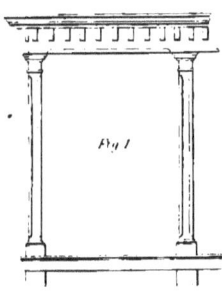

Fig 1

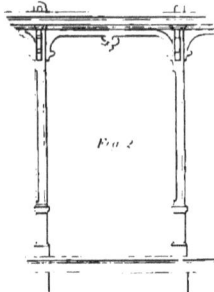

Fig 2

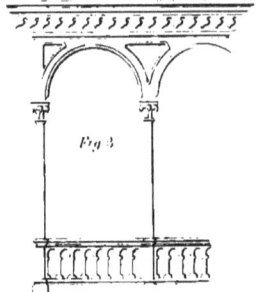

Fig 3

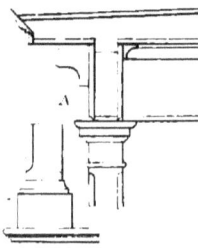

A

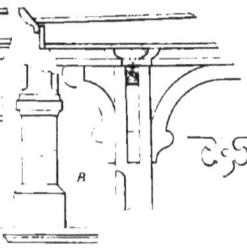

B

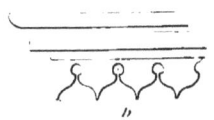

b

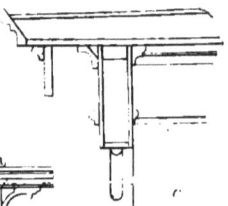

c

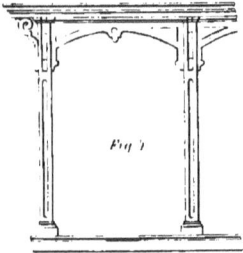

Fig 4

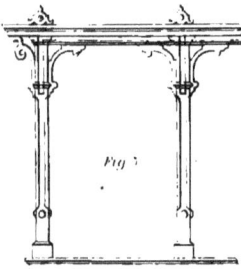

Fig 5

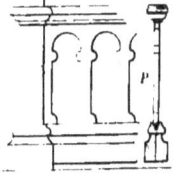

P

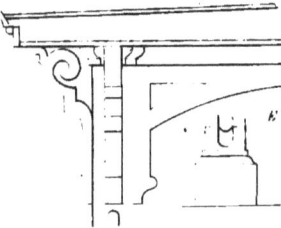

H

PLATE 35.

Fig. 1. Has square columns, chamfered at the corners, and having moulded capitals and bases. The cornice has sawed blocks 3 inches thick. At A are the details.

Figs. 2, 3, and 4. Have square columns with chamfered corners and moulded bases. The frieze to each consists of sawed-work 3 inches thick, and the brackets are of the same thickness. B shows the details of Fig. 2; F, those of Fig. 3; and E, those of Fig. 4.

Fig. 5. Has chamfered columns from which spring brackets 3 inches thick Over the columns are scrolls 3 inches thick, placed on the roof.

These piazzas are simple in their construction, neat in appearance and are appropriate for small cottages of moderate cost.

Fig. 6. Has turned columns 4 inches in diameter, with carved capitals, and moulded base. The frieze is arched and panelled, and the soffits are moulded. The cornice has a verge-board, sawed from 2-inch plank. The railing is of sawed-work 1¼ inch thick, having moulded cap and base. C shows the columns and cornice; D, the verge-board; and P, a section of the railing.

The designs are drawn ¼ inch to a foot, and the details ⅞ of an inch to a foot.

PLATE 36.

Fig. 1. Shows enlarged drawing of veranda of house on Plate 49, Drawing B. The main columns or piers are 12 inches square, worked with moulded edges. The smaller columns are round, 4 inches in diameter, with carved capital. The upper and lower balustrades are made of 1½-inch plank sawed in the patterns as illustrated, with moulded cap and plain bevelled base. This design is an illustration of a very expensive, elaborate, broad veranda, and is very suitable for a broad plain front.

Fig. 2. Shows veranda with lower balustrade made of turned balusters 5 inches square at the base, with moulded rail. The columns are 8 inches square with bevelled corners. Details D, show sections lower balustrade, and section through cornice showing bracket; F shows modillion between large brackets; E, section of column; H shows section through pedestal of lower balustrade; G shows upper balustrade.

Fig. 3. Columns of veranda similar to Fig. 2. The columns are placed farther apart, and an arch sprung between the columns; this arch-piece is made of 3-inch plank with bevelled edges. Drawings A and C show section of column, base of column, and section through cornice.

Fig. 1 is drawn on the scale of ½ an inch to a foot; Figs. 2 and 3, on the scale of ¼ of an inch to a foot. Details C, D, E, F, G, and H, on the scale of ¾ of an inch to a foot.

Plate 36

Fig 3

Fig 2

Fig 1

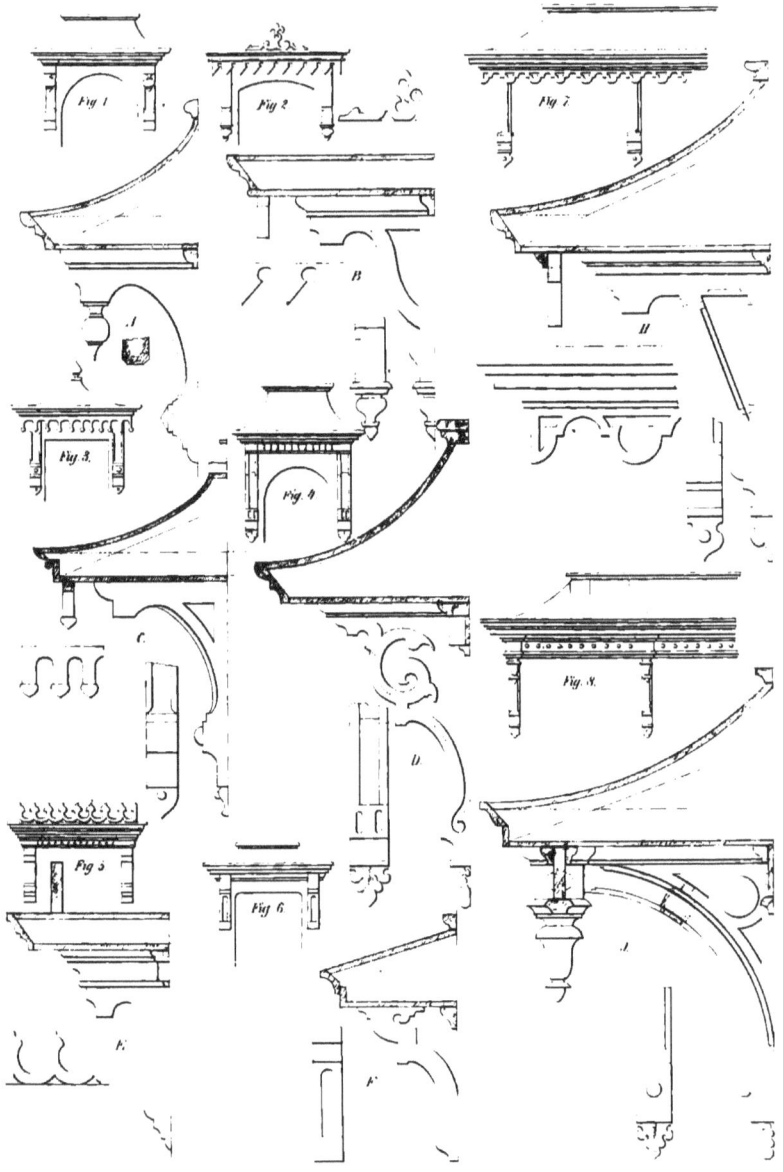

Fig. 1
Fig. 2
Fig. 7
Fig. 3
Fig. 4
Fig. 5
Fig. 6
Fig. 8

PLATE 37.

These canopies have projecting roofs, curved or flat, and variously ornamented, and are supported by brackets of various patterns.

Fig. 1. Has a curved roof, with a bold moulding at the top of its curve. The brackets are 5 inches thick, and are bevelled on the face, and have turned pendants at the top, and raised pieces at the bottom. The details are shown at A.

Fig. 2. Has a flat roof, ornamented with a scroll 4 inches thick. The cornice is moulded and has a sawed verge-board, 2 inches thick. The brackets are plain, and are 5 inches thick, and have turned corbels at the foot. At B are the details.

Fig. 3. Has a curved roof with a turned finial at the top. The cornice has a verge-board 1½ inches thick, sawed in the form of a series of small arches, and these have turned drops. The brackets are 5 inches thick, and have sawed foot-leaves. The details are shown at C.

Fig. 4. Has a curved roof, moulded at the top. The cornice is also moulded and has plain dentils, placed between the brackets. The brackets are 6 inches thick and scroll sawed from three thicknesses of plank, and have raised mouldings and carved leaves at the bottom. At D are the details.

Fig. 5. Has a flat roof, ornamented with a balustrade, sawed from 2-inch plank. The brackets are plain and 4 inches thick; between them are sawed dentils 2½ inches thick. At E are the details. Fig. 6 shows a plain canopy. At F are the details. Figs. 7 and 8 show canopies which are designed to cover two or more openings. At H and J are the details.

The designs are ¼ inch to the foot, and the details ¾ inch to the foot.

PLATE 38.

DESIGNS FOR AN ENTRANCE DOOR, BAY WINDOW, AND DOOR-CAPS.

Fig. 1. Shows a doorway having a straight moulded cap, supported by carved trusses and sawed dentil-blocks, and surmounted by a sawed scroll. The pilasters are chamfered at the corners, and the jambs are moulded. An elevation is shown at A, a section at B, and a section of the pilasters, jambs and doors at C.

Fig. 4. Shows a bay window having panelled pilasters with pedestals; between the pedestals are half balusters. The cornice has sawed modillions, placed in pairs. The roof balustrade has panelled pedestals, and railings with turned balusters. D shows the cornice, E the balustrade, F the sections of the pilasters and box-frames, and G a section of the finish under the windows.

Figs. 2 and 3, Show designs for door-hoods, supported by sawed brackets 3 inches thick.

Fig. 5 Shows a design for a window-cap.

The elevations of door and bay window are drawn $\frac{1}{4}$ inch to the foot. All other drawings on this Plate are $\frac{3}{4}$ inch to a foot.

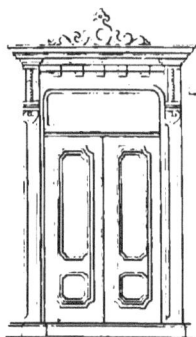

Fig 1.

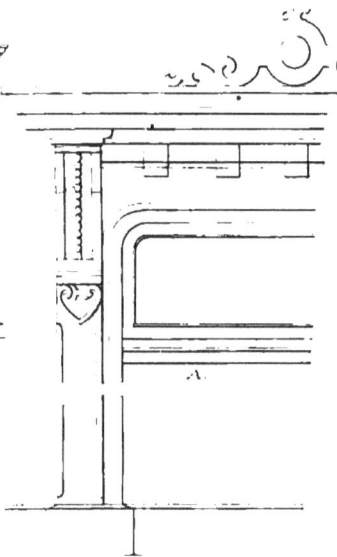

A.

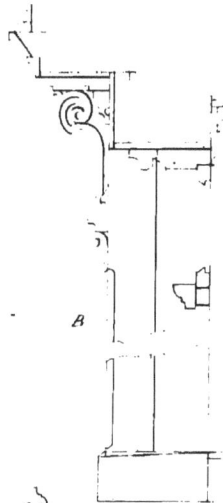

B.

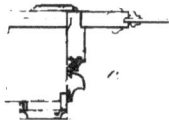

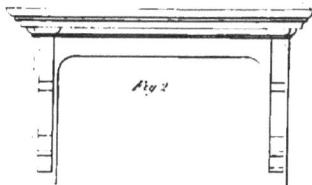

Fig 2

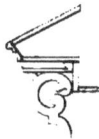

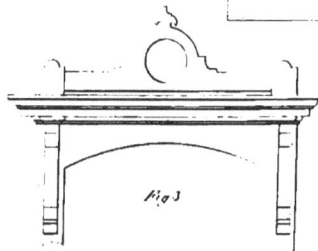

Fig 3

Fig 4

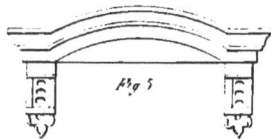

Fig 5

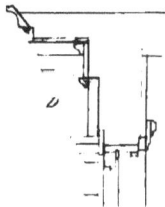

D.

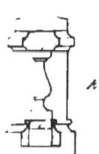

E.

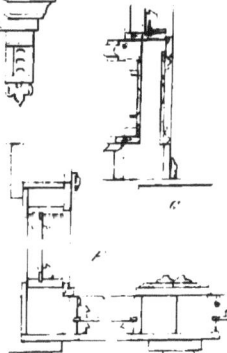

Plate 39

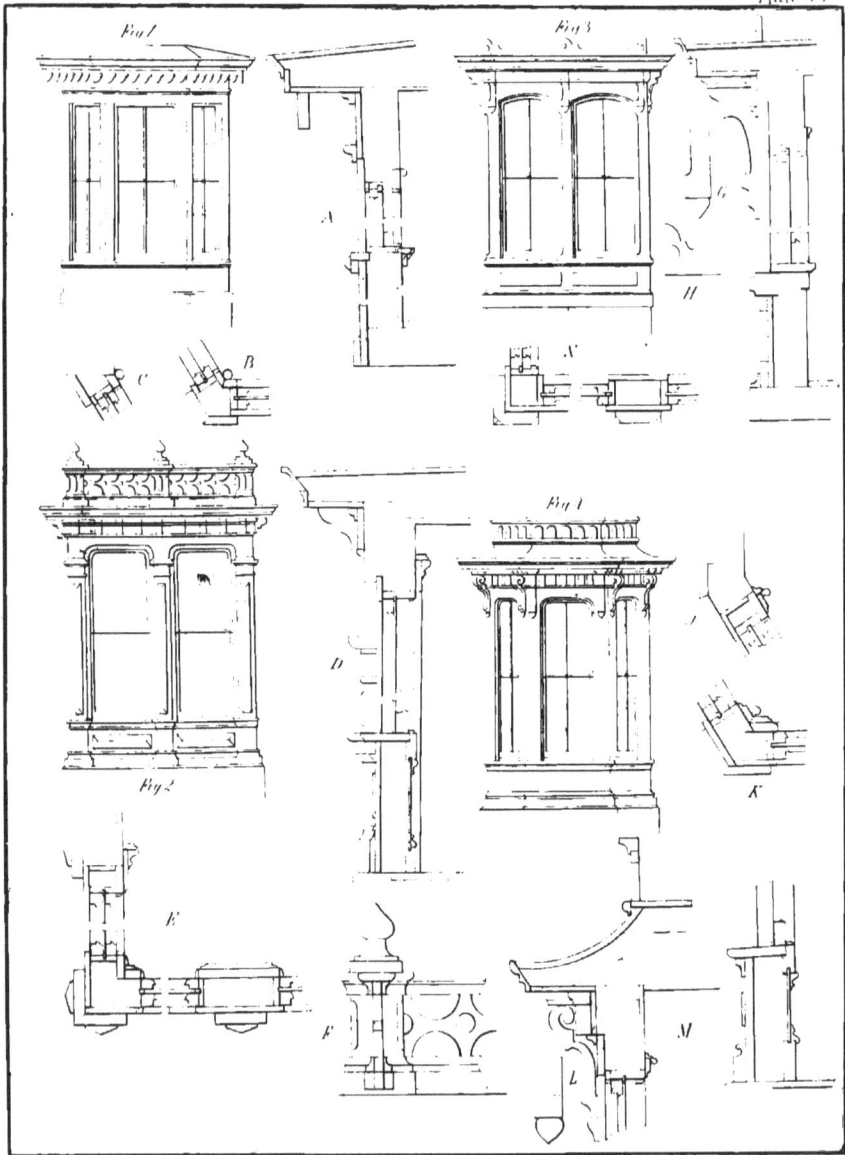

Fig 1

Fig 3

Fig 2

Fig 4

PLATE 39

Fig. 1. Has a cornice, with sawed verge-board, plain pilasters, and moulded sills and base. A shows a section of the cornice and the finish under the windows. B one of the angle-boxes, and C one of the wall-boxes.

Fig. 2. Has panelled pilasters; standing under them are moulded pedestals, and between these are panels. The cornice has arched frieze and small sawed brackets. The roof railing has fluted pedestals and open sawed work. D shows the details of the cornice, pilasters, and work under the windows, E the wall, corner, and centre boxes, F the railing on the roof.

Fig. 3. Has pilasters with chamfered corners. The frieze is arched and the cornice has sawed and bevelled brackets. The balustrade is of 1½-inch plank, and under the windows are plain panels and moulded sills and base. N shows the angle and centre boxes, G the cornice and work under the windows, and H the balustrade.

Fig. 4. Has plain pilasters, arched frieze, and a cornice with scroll brackets and plain dentils; under the windows are moulded sills and base. The roof is curved over the cornice, and at the top is a railing of sawed work, 2 inches thick. At L is a section of the cornice, at M a section of the finish under the windows, and at J and K are the wall and angle boxes.

The designs are ¼ inch to the foot, and the details ¾ inch to the foot.

PLATE 40.

The observatories shown on this Plate are intended to be used on buildings two or more stories in height, and should be placed in the centre of the roofs. Where observatories are used, the roofs should be hipped, and should not have a pitch of more than 1 foot in 2 feet. The observatories should be square in plan, and their width should be about ¼ the width of the front of the building on which they are placed.

Fig. 1. Has a cornice with dentils and sawed brackets, 6 inches thick, also a moulded base and foot-brackets, placed under those of the cornice and extending down the roof of the building : on the cornice is a scroll 4 inches thick, and at the apex of the roof a finial, consisting of four scrolls, placed around a 4×4 inch centre-stick, having a turned top. At A is a section of the cornice; at B, a section of the base and lower brackets, and at C, the roof scroll and finial.

Fig. 2. Has upper and lower sawed brackets, placed in pairs, a moulded base, a cornice with a small gable in the centre and sawed dentils between the brackets and a roof-finial with centre-stick and four scrolls. D shows a detail of the cornice, E the base and lower brackets, and F the finial.

Fig. 3. Represents an observatory elaborate in detail; it should be used on a building in which the curved roof is used. The cornice has brackets, with carved leaves, placed in pairs ; between the brackets are sawed dentils, and under the frieze are moulded corbels. At the corners are pilasters which terminate at the frieze The top of the roof is flat and has a railing of sawed work, having pedestals surmounted by turned urns. In the curved roof are dormer windows with circular sash. Around the observatory is a railing, having turned balusters and panelled pedestals with turned urns. K shows the cornice, G, the upper railing, H, the lower railing, and J, the dormer windows.

Plate 40

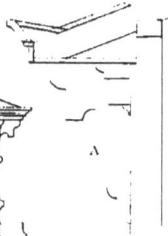

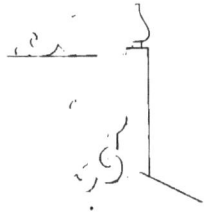

Fig 1

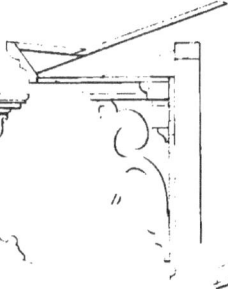

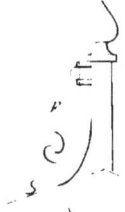

Fig 2

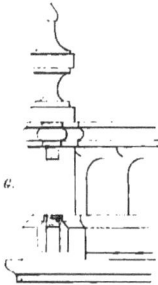

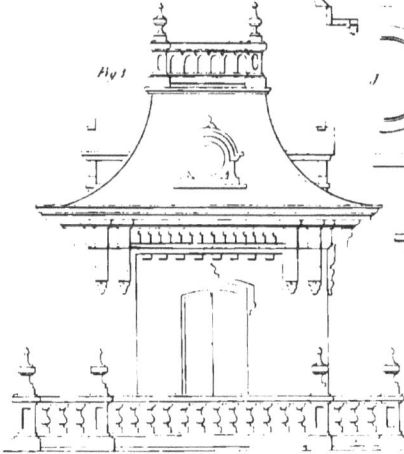

Fig 3

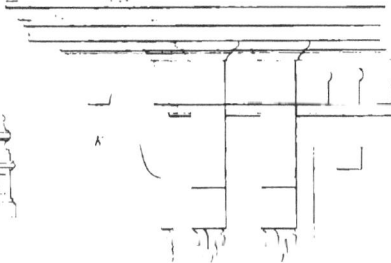

Plate 44

Fig. 1

Fig. 2

Fig. 3

Fig. 4

Fig. 5

Fig. 6

Fig. 7

Fig. 8

Fig. 9

Fig. 10

Fig. 11

A

B

C

D

E

F

G

H

PLATE 41.

Figures 1, 2, 3, 4, 5, 6, 10, and 11. Show details of railings suitable for balconies and verandas. All have moulded caps and bases. The ornamental work or "filling in" is made of sawed plank, ranging in thickness from 1 inch to 2 inches—2-inch plank sawed for the "filling in" has a much better effect, and looks more substantial.

Fig. 7. Design of balcony intended to be placed over entrance-doorway. The balustrade is 2 feet 6 inches high. Projection of balcony from line of wall, 3 feet 5 inches—not including projection of cornice. The brackets supporting balcony are 8 inches thick. See drawings A and B for section of balcony and details enlarged.

Fig. 8. Design of balcony for similar location as the above—balcony rail 2 feet 6 inches high—little columns 2 inches in diameter, with arches springing from top of columns, made of 2-inch plank—and back of columns and arches the "filling in" of circle and cross to be of inch stuff. For enlargement and section see drawing, represented at D.

Fig. 9. Balcony similar to the preceding two designs, with a balcony rail made of 2-inch plank, and the pattern placed edge-wise, as shown by the section F. Drawing F shows side of bracket, and drawing G the face. Figs. 7, 8, and 9 are on the scale of 1 of an inch to a foot; and the illustrations of these, enlarged, are ¼ an inch to a foot.

PLATE 42.

DESIGNS FOR BALCONIES, DORMER WINDOWS, GABLE SCROLLS, &C.

Figs. 1, 2, 3, and 4. Show balconies for windows: they may be placed in front of one opening only, or they may be made of sufficient length to include two or more openings. All these balconies are to be supported by brackets. The railing in Fig. 1. is of sawed work; that in Figs. 2, 3, and 4, is of turned balusters. The pedestals are panelled and chamfered, and those of Fig. 4 have turned urns. Figs. 5, 6, and 7 show dormer windows, suitable for steep roofs. At A, B, C, are the details of Fig. 5; at E, F, G, the details of Fig. 6; and at J, K, L, the details of Fig. 7. M shows a sawed balustrade to be used on flat roofs. N shows a window cap. Figs. 8 and 9, gable scrolls, which should be 4 inches thick. Fig. 10 shows a chimney top designed to be constructed of brick with a moulded stone cap.

The details on this plate are drawn $\frac{3}{4}$ inch to a foot, and the designs $\frac{1}{4}$ inch to a foot.

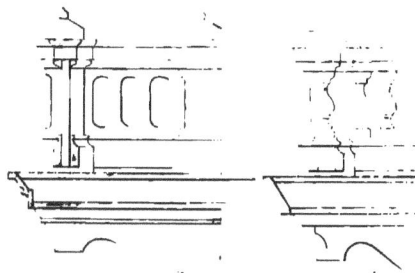

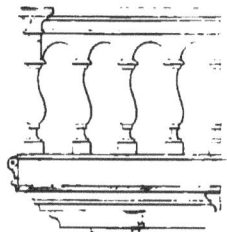

Fig 1

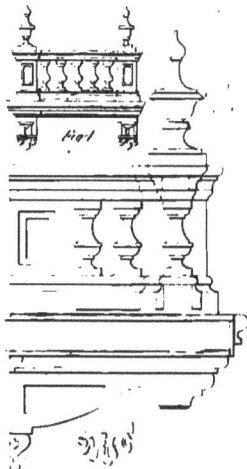

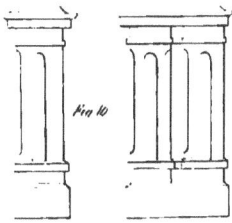

Fig 10

Fig 5

Fig 6

Fig 8

Fig 7

Fig 9

B

D

A'

A

N

K

Plate 45

PLATE 43.

Designs of chimney caps. Bases and caps are of brick and stone.

Design A represents a cluster of chimneys, three in number, each shaft 16 inches square, and placed 4 inches apart.

Design B represents two shafts, 16 inches square, and placed 8 inches apart.

Design C shows a panelled chimney shaft, 4 feet broad by 20 inches thick. The panels are sunk 2 inches.

Designs D, E, F, are designs of stone chimney caps. Also the moulded bases to be of stone. The shafts can be of stone or brick.

Designs G, H, and I, are designs of brick chimneys. Design G, the shafts are 20 inches square, placed 8 inches apart. Design H is 3 feet broad on the face, and 20 inches thick, with brick pilasters 8 inches wide on the corners, and sunk panel in the centre. The pilasters project beyond the face of chimney shaft 2 inches, and the panel in the centre is sunk 2 inches.

Design J is a couplet chimney; shafts 16 inches square, with brick cap and base.

All of these designs are drawn on the scale of ½ an inch to a foot.

PLATE 44.

Fig. 1. Design of plain stairs, with 7-inch rise, and 10-inch tread; size of newel at the base, 10 inches square. Balusters 2½ inches square at the base; the balusters are turned. The newel is an octagon shaft; it can be turned if desirable. See drawing A, for nosing of stairs and brackets enlarged.

Fig. 2. Design of stairs, 7-inch rise, 10-inch tread. The newel is 12 inches square at the base, carved shaft, octagon in plan. Drawing B shows bracket of stairs enlarged. The balusters are 2½ inches square at the base, turned with octagon shaft.

Figs. 3 and 4. Two designs for newel posts and balusters; each of the newels are 12 inches square at the base.

Fig. 5. Design of stairs; 6½-inch rise, 11-inch tread. The newel is turned, and a part of it carved, and is 10 inches square at the base. The main balusters are 3 inches square, turned; the smaller balusters are turned, 1¾ inches in diameter. The square panel between the large balusters is moulded with a fillit and cove, and a carved ornament in the centre. For enlargement of brackets, see drawing C.

Fig. 6. Design of stairs, 6-inch rise and 12-inch tread. Newel 10 inches square at the base, carved. Balusters 3 inches square at the base, carved, and a part turned; in place of the bracket is a panel.

Fig. 7. Design for first-class stair case; the risers are 6 inches, treads 11 inches. The newel is 12 inches square at the base, carved. The balusters are octagon, 3 inches in diameter, turned at the top and the bottom. The ornament between balusters is made of inch stuff; the brackets are plain.

Sections at E, G, and F, are sections of hand rails. These drawings are all made on the scale of ⅞ths of an inch to a foot, except the drawings of the enlargement of brackets, and the sections of rails at E, G, and F, which are 1½ inch to a foot.

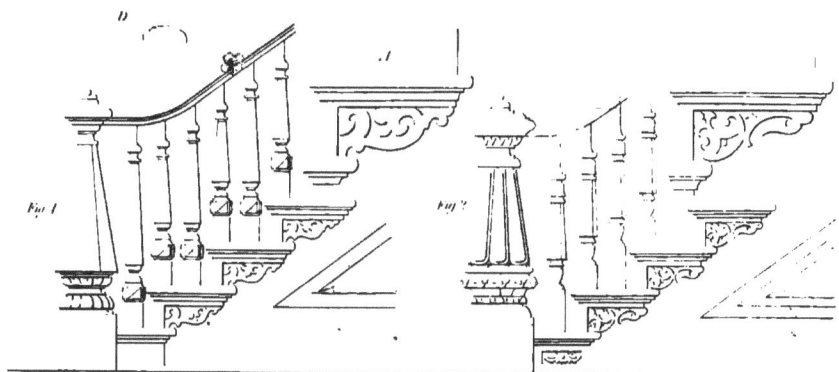

Fig. 1

Fig. 2

Fig. 3

Fig. 4

Fig. 5

Fig. 6

Fig. 7

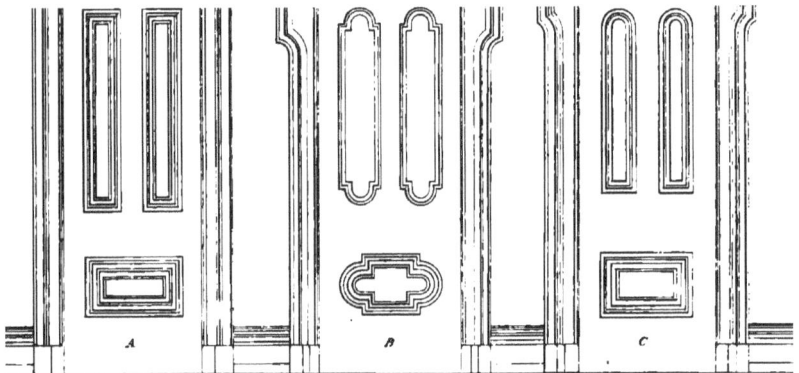

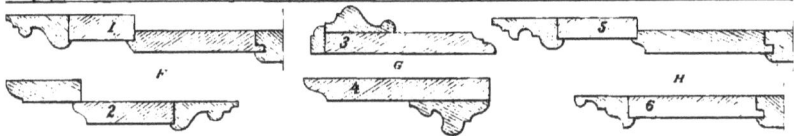

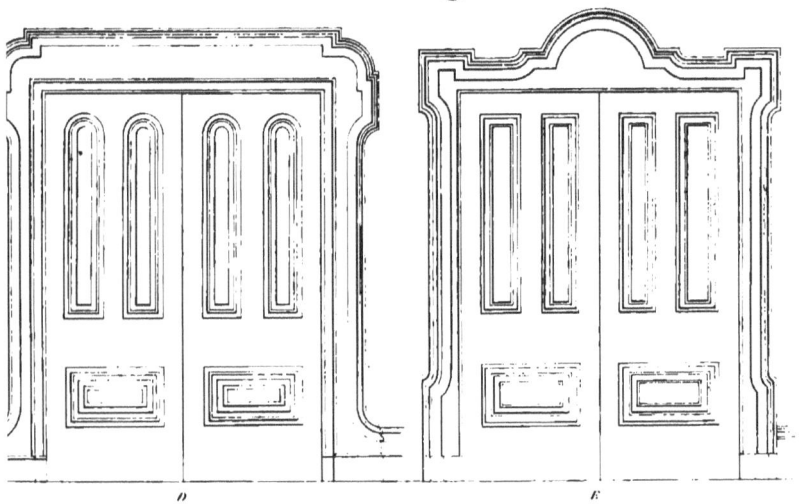

PLATE 45.

Designs A, B, C, D, and E, are styles of finish for first-class houses. Any mouldings on Plate 47 can be used for this irregular finish. The moulded face casing, section at F, is the moulding of doorway D; and the section above, the face casing, is section of the base. The sections at G are examples of face casing mouldings, or architraves for doors and windows. Sections at H are both base mouldings.

Designs D and E are double or sliding doors. The panels for the doors should have raised mouldings.

These designs are drawn on the scale of ½ an inch to a foot. The sections of finish are on the scale of 3 inches to a foot.

PLATE 46.

Fig. 1. Shows a section of a window. At A are the inside blinds, closed. B shows the blinds folded into the box prepared for their reception. C, the inside casing or architrave. D, the outside casing of 2-inch plank.

Fig. 2. Is a section of the lower part of the window, showing the finish from the sill to the floor. E is the panelled back. F, the panelled elbow under the blinds, where folded into the box. G, the outside or sub-sill; and H, the sill of the window-frame. This window is designed to be used in a frame building.

Fig. 3. Is a section of a window, showing the frame, inside shutters, pockets or boxes, and the inside finish. J shows the shutters, when closed. K, one half of the shutters folded into a box, or pocket, so that they stand at right angles to the window. L, the shutters folded into a splayed box or pocket. M, the box of the window-frame in which the weights are placed; and N, the outside or face of the wall. Where inside shutters or blinds are folded into pockets, it becomes necessary to set studs or framing, separate from the walls, in order to get the depth or width of the jambs sufficient to receive the shutters.

The scale of these drawings is 1½ inches to a foot.

Plate 46

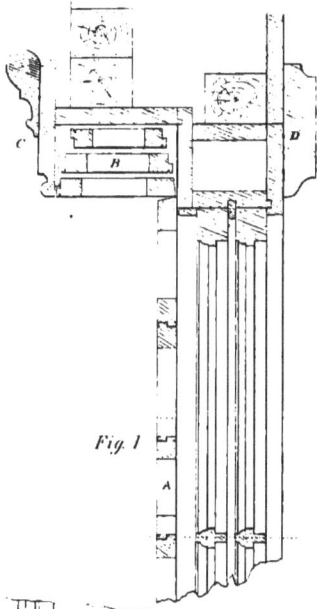

Fig. 1

Fig. 2

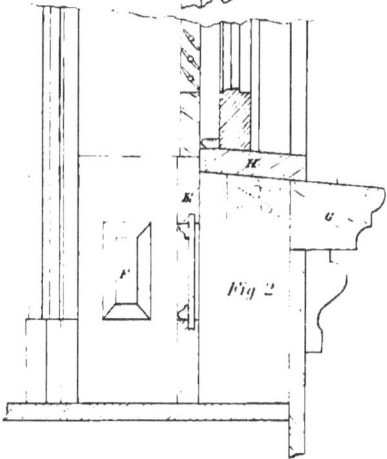

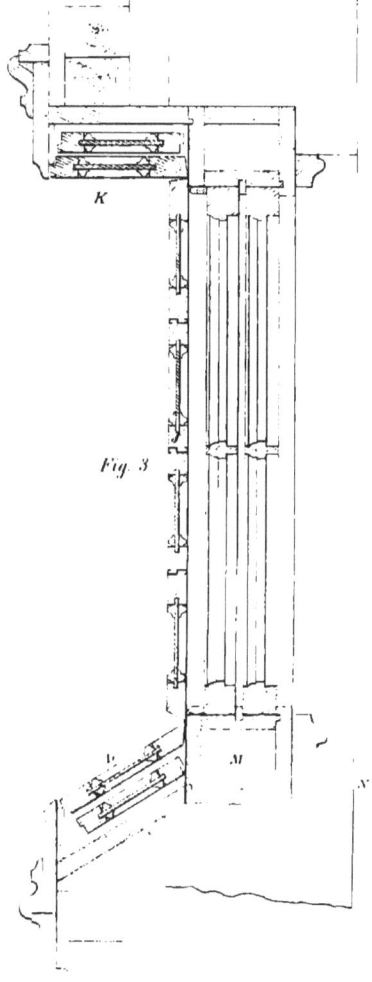

Fig. 3

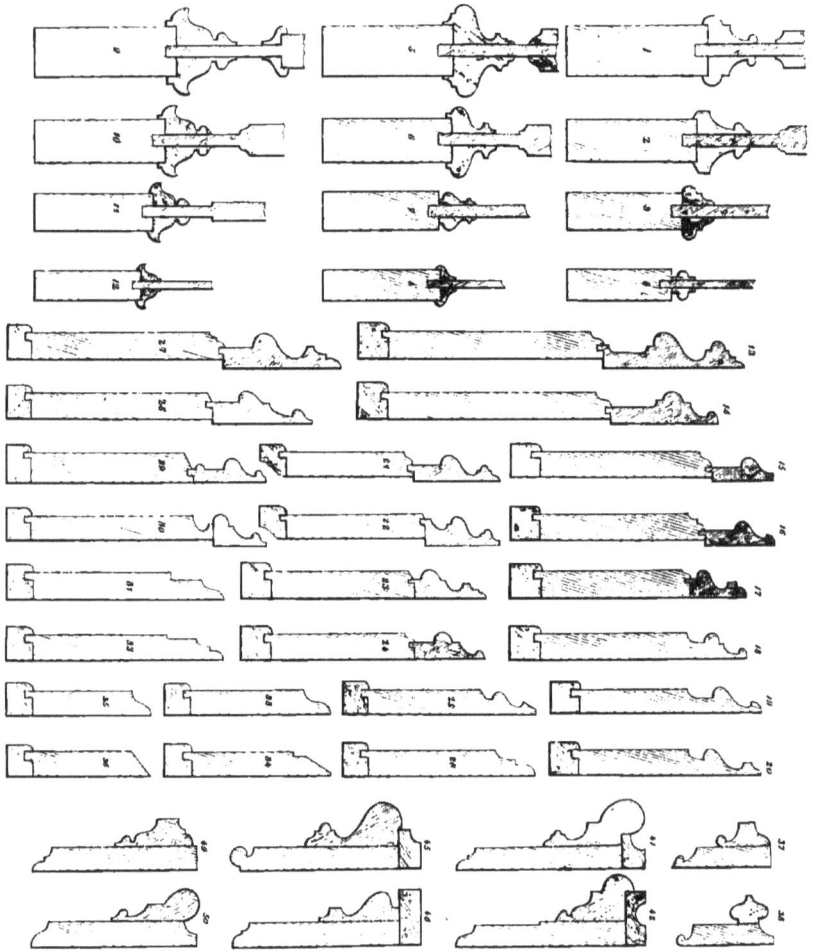

PLATE 47.

Sections of casing, or architraves for the inside of doors and windows. Skirting, or base, and door stiles, panels and mouldings.

The sections of casing range in width from 3 inches to 8 inches, and variously moulded.

The sections of skirting or base, show designs from 5 inches to 15 inches high, and comprise a variety of style, from a plain bevelled example to an elaborate design. All wide base-boards should be tongued into the floor, or into strips.

The sections of the doors vary from 1½ inches thick to 2 inches, and show raised and sunk mouldings, and raised and plain panels.

The scale of these drawings is 3 inches to a foot.

PLATE 48.

Figs. 1, 2, and 3. Designs of ornamental picket fences. The pickets are intended to be made of inch stuff. The posts of Fig. 1 are 6 inches square. Fig. 2, post, 8 inches square. Fig. 3, post, 12 inches square. In these 3 designs, the height of fence from ground to top of picket is 3 feet 10 inches.

Fig. 4. Is a design for a fence where the post only comes up out the ground about the height of the base-board. The base put on, and capped with 1½-inch boards, as shown in section. The pickets are sawed in pattern, as shown in section ; they are 8 inches wide, and are placed crosswise ; and in the front view of fence only the edge of the picket is seen. These pickets should be at least 1½ inches thick. The " filling in," or ornamental pattern at the top and bottom, between pickets, may be made of inch stuff. The pickets are sawed to fit the top of base, and can be strongly nailed. The manner of putting on the cap can be easily understood by referring to the section. This fence is perfectly water-proof. The shaft of the post is 18 inches square

Fig. 5. Design of fence made of standards 4 × 4 inches square, filled in with diagonal cross-pieces 2 × 4 inches. The wheel to be made of stuff 2 inches thick, ornamental points in centre. of 2-inch stuff. Posts in the ground should be placed to fit the standards in the fence, and the support from posts for the fence to be obtained by means of ½-inch rod from ground post, through standards above posts, and screwed fast by means of nut and washer above top rail. The main corner or gate-posts of this fence are 18 inches square, with sunk panel. Top of posts finished with moulded cap and turned ball, finial or vase.

Fig. 6. Is a design of turned baluster fence, with some carving on the balusters. The balusters are 6 inches square at the base. Post 18 inches square, finished with steep-roofed cap.

Fig. 7. Design of fence, similar in construction to design or Fig. 4. The cross-pickets are placed a greater distance apart, and the filling in made in a larger pattern and different manner.

All of these designs are drawn on the scale of ⅜ths of an inch to a foot

Plate 18

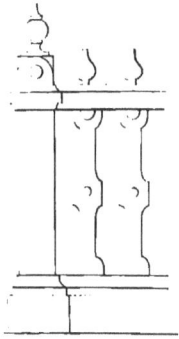

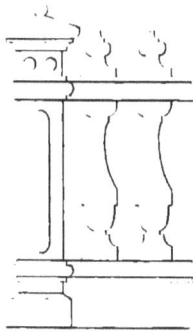

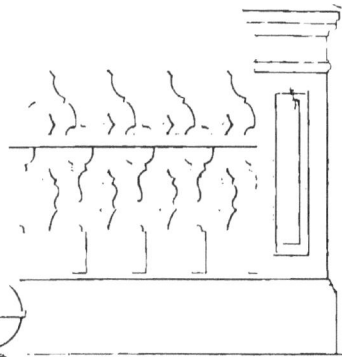

Fig 1

Fig 2

Fig 3

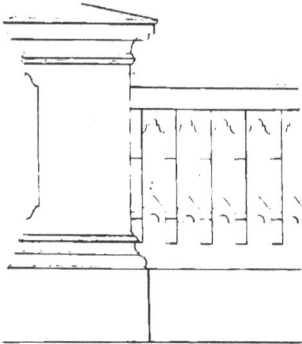

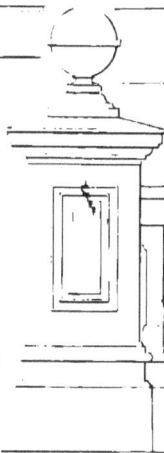

Fig 4

Fig 5

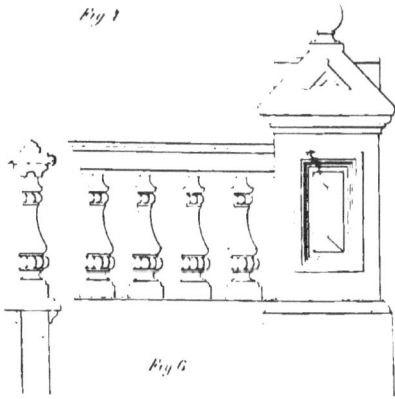

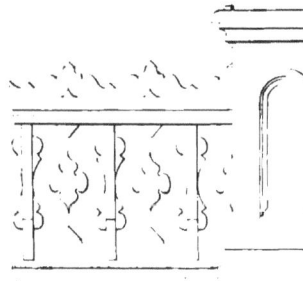

Fig 6

Fig 7

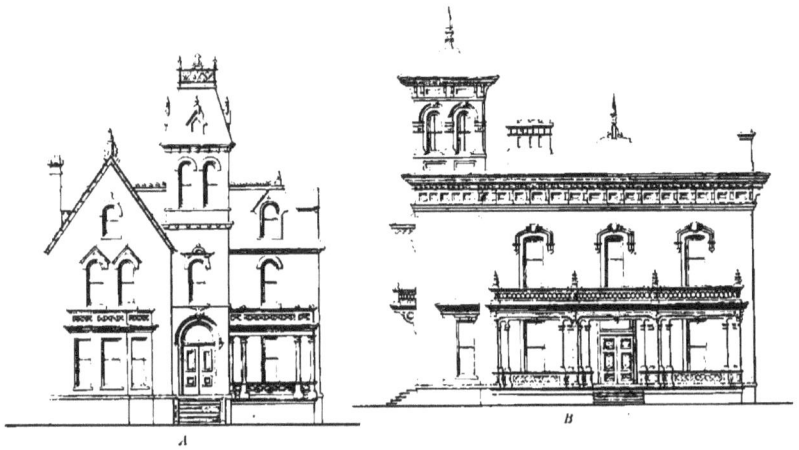

A

B

C

PLATE 49.

Design A. Shows an elevation of a house; the plan, the form of the letter L, with a tower in the angle. The roofs have a steep pitch; the main part with a gable in front; the other roof is a French roof with a flat on top. Dormer windows introduced in the roof for finishing, and lighting chambers, if required in the attic. The bay window is large and commodious, 14 feet across, outside dimensions. Front door 6 feet wide, with cut stone cap or arch; also cut stone caps for windows. The veranda is designed to be built of wood.

Design B. Is a design of a large house, 47 feet square, with a tower 12 feet square, placed in the middle of the left flank elevation, and bay windows introduced on each side of tower. The veranda is shown in detail on Plate 36, Fig. 1. The balcony on the tower is shown in Plate 41, Fig 7. The cornice has 3 feet projection, and is about 5 feet high, with sunk panels between the brackets; cornice of tower has 3 feet projection and is 4 feet high; brackets placed in pairs, with sunk panels between them.

Design C. Shows an elevation of a house, square in plan, and having a centre projection to the front. The roofs, dormers and cornice, are shown on Plate 28; the observatory and railing at Fig. 3, Plate 40; the window finish on Plate 31; the bay window at Fig. 1, Plate 38; the side piazza and front porch, at Fig. 1, Plate 33; and the balconies at Fig. 4, Plate 42.

These designs are for large houses of an elaborate character, and may be executed in wood or brick. If brick is used, the door and window finish should be executed in stone.

Designs A and B are drawn on the scale of 16 feet to an inch. Design C is drawn on the scale of 12 feet to an inch.

PLATE 50.

Fig. 2. Shows a design for a house which should be square in plan, having a hall in the centre. Figs. 1, 3, 4, and 6, show elevations for houses, having a front of from 20 feet to 30 feet, and a hall on one side. Fig. 5 shows an elevation of a house with a main building and a wing, with the hall between the two.

Figs. 1 and 3. Have steep or curved roofs, which should be covered with slate or shingles. These houses are three stories in height, and the rooms in the upper story are lighted by dormer windows, placed in the steep roofs.

The cornice of Fig. 1, is shown at Fig. 8, Plate 24; the finish of the doors and windows at Fig. 10, Plate 14, and Fig. 2, Plate 31; and the dormer window at Fig. 1, Plate 27.

The cornice of Fig. 2, is shown at Fig. 2, Plate 27: the porch at Fig. 3, Plate 32; and the railing on the roof at Fig. 1, Plate 28. The windows have plain spring and key stones.

The dormer windows of Fig. 3, are shown at Fig. 2, Plate 27: the cornice at Fig. 2, Plate 27; the windows at Figs. 21 and 23, Plate 13: door and finish at Fig. 9, Plate 14; and the piazzas at Fig. 1, Plate 35.

The cornice of Fig. 4, is shown at Fig. 1, Plate 25: the balustrade of the roof at Fig. M, Plate 42; the windows at Fig. 23, Plate 13; and the piazza at Fig. 4, Plate 25.

The observatory of Fig. 5, is shown at Fig. 1, Plate 40; the cornices at Fig. 1, Plate 37; the window-caps at Fig. 1, Plate 27: the door-cap at Fig. 3, Plate 38; the piazza at Fig. 3, Plate 33; the window canopy at Fig. 1, Plate 27; and the balconies at Fig. 3, Plate 42.

The cornice of Fig. 6, is shown at Fig. 2, Plate 25; the window-caps at Fig. 4 Plate 31; the porch at Fig. 1, Plate 32; the piazza at Fig. 2, Plate 35: the bay window at Fig. 1, Plate 39; and the balconies at Fig. 2, Plate 42.

The roofs in Figs. 4, 5, and 6, should be covered with tin, shingles or slate: where tin is used the joints should be raised and locked together.

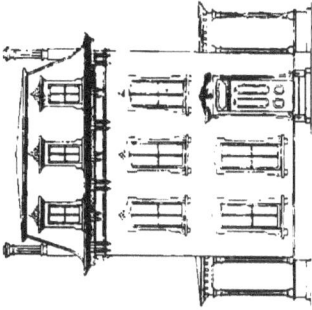

Fig. 3

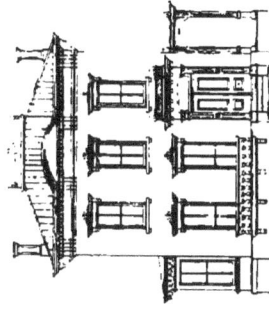

Fig. 6

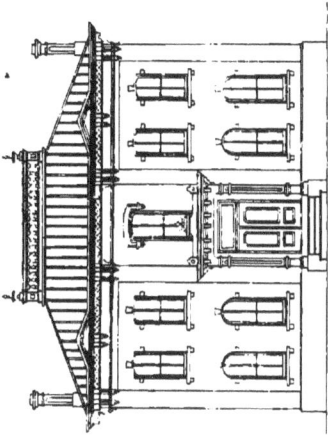

Fig. 2

Fig. 5

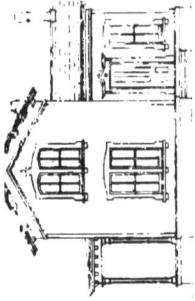

Fig 3.

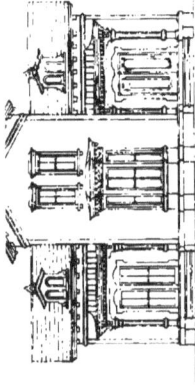

Fig 2.

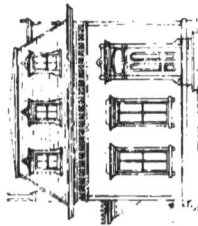

Fig 1.

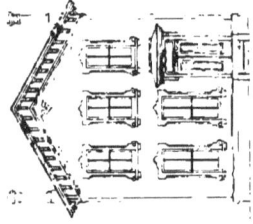

Fig 6.

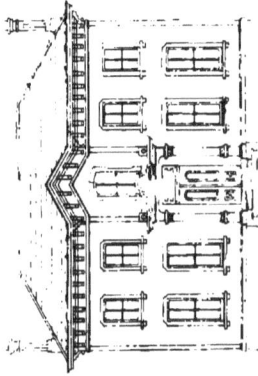

Fig 5.

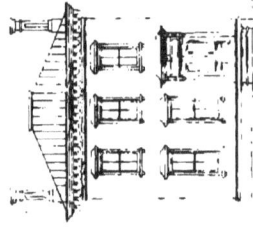

Fig 4.

PLATE 51.

Fig. 1. Shows a design for a cottage with a steep roof, with dormer windows to light the second story. The dormer windows are shown at Fig. 2, Plate 27, the cornice at Fig. 7, Plate 24; the window-caps, and that of the door at Figs. 2 and 3, Plate 38; the canopy at Fig. 5, Plate 37; and the balcony at Fig. 1, Plate 42.

Fig. 2. Shows a design for a cottage, having a centre portion two stories high, with a wing on each side, one story and a half high. The half story in the wings would be lighted by the dormer windows. The cornices are shown at Fig. 12, Plate 26; dormer windows at Fig. 6, Plate 42; second story windows at Fig. 11 Plate 31; windows in the wings at Fig. 13, Plate 13; piazzas at Fig. 3, Plate 33 and the bay window at Fig. 1, Plate 39.

Fig. 3. Shows a cottage with a wing on one side The cornices are shown at Fig 5, Plate 26; the window finish at Figs. 13 and 26, Plate 13; the door-cap at Fig. 9, Plate 14; and the piazza at Fig. 1, Plate 35.

Fig. 4. Shows an elevation of a small two story dwelling house. The cornice is shown at Fig. 6, Plate 24; the window-caps at Fig. 11, Plate 31; and the door-cap at Fig. 6, Plate 31.

Fig. 5. Shows an elevation of a house that should be square in plan, with the hall in the centre. The cornice is shown at Fig. 15, Plate 26; the windows at Fig. 12, Plate 13; and the porch at Fig. 5, Plate 32.

Fig. 6. Shows an elevation of a two story cottage. The cornice is shown at Fig. 17, Plate 26; the windows at Fig 21, Plate 13; and the door-cap at Fig. 11, Plate 31.

The designs on this Plate should be executed in wood; but Figs. 1 and 4 may have walls of brick, and trimmings of wood.

PLATE 52.

Fig. 1. Shows the front of a cottage having a wing, in which is placed the front entrance door. The cornice is shown at Fig. 3, Plate 30; the windows at Fig. 13, Plate 13; the bay window at Fig 3, Plate 39, and the porch at Fig. 2. Plate 33.

Fig. 2. Shows the front of a house which should be square in plan; the centre portion of the front should project about 2 feet from the balance of the front. The cornice and the finish of the gables is shown at Fig. 4, Plate 30; the ridge ornament at Fig. M, Plate 42; the windows at Fig. 6, Plate 13; the porch at Fig. 3, Plate 32; the bay window at Fig. 4, Plate 39; the canopy at Fig. 3. Plate 37; and the balcony at Fig. 2, Plate 42.

The cornice of the cottage shown in Fig. 3 is detailed at Fig. 5. Plate 30; the first story windows at Fig. 11, Plate 31; the front-door hood at Fig. 11, Plate 31; the piazza at Fig. 5. Plate 35; the bay window at Fig. 1. Plate 39; and the balcony at Fig. 2, Plate 42. The balcony of first story windows is shown at Fig. 2, Plate 42; and the canopy over the second story windows at Fig. 2, Plate 37.

The cornice and gable finish of Fig. 4 is shown at Fig. 1, Plate 30; the canopy at Fig. 1, Plate 37; the piazza at Fig. 1, Plate 35; and the window finish and that of the door at Fig. 24, Plate 13.

Fig. 5. Shows a design of a house that should be square in plan, with a centre projection in front. The cornice is shown at Fig. 3, Plate 30; the dormer windows at Fig. 5, Plate 42; the gable window at Fig. 1, Plate 14; the caps of the lower windows and that of the entrance door at Fig. 8, Plate 14; and the piazza at Fig. 5, Plate 35.

Fig. 6. Shows an elevation of a cottage irregular in plan; that portion of the front surmounted by the gable, should project a foot from the balance of the front. The cornice is shown at Fig. 2, Plate 30; the dormer windows at Fig. 7 Plate 42; the railing on the roof at Fig. 3, Plate 14; the window-caps at Fig. 7 Plate 14; the porch at Fig. 2, Plate 32; and the piazza at Fig. 1, Plate 35.

Figs. 2 and 5 would look well if the walls were of rough stone; but wood would be a proper material in which to execute all the designs shown on this Plate.

Plate 52

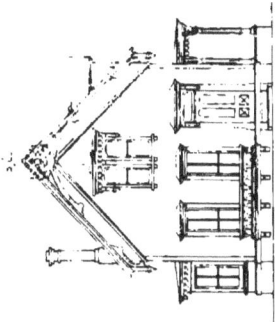

Fig. 3

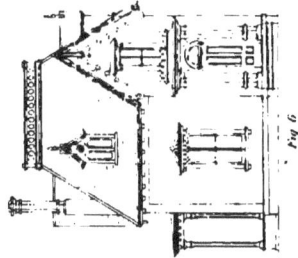

Fig. 6

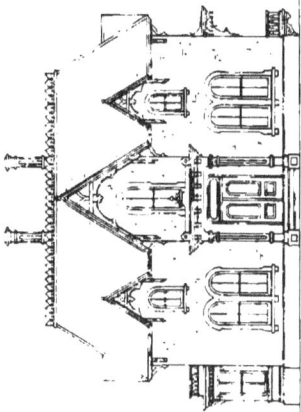

Fig. 2

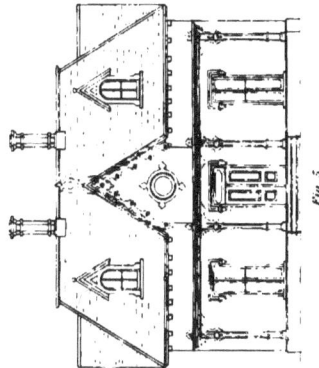

Fig. 5

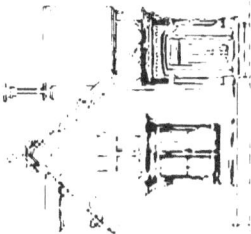

Fig. 1

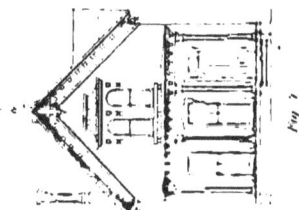

Fig. 4

www.ingramcontent.com/pod-product-compliance
Lightning Source LLC
Chambersburg PA
CBHW020556270326
41927CB00006B/858